D1103760

The Salvation Army
School For Officers' Training
Library
Chicago, Illinois

# WOLFHART PANNENBERG

*Makers of the Modern Theological Mind*

**Bob E. Patterson, Editor**

KARL BARTH by *David L. Mueller*
DIETRICH BONHOEFFER by *Dallas M. Roark*
RUDOLF BULTMANN by *Morris Ashcraft*
CHARLES HARTSHORNE by *Alan Gragg*
WOLFHART PANNENBERG by *Don Olive*
TEILHARD DE CHARDIN by *Doran McCarty*
EMIL BRUNNER by *J. Edward Humphrey*
MARTIN BUBER by *Stephen M. Panko*
SÖREN KIERKEGAARD by *Elmer H. Duncan*
REINHOLD NIEBUHR by *Bob E. Patterson*
H. RICHARD NIEBUHR by *Lonnie D. Kliever*
GERHARD VON RAD by *James L. Crenshaw*
ANDERS NYGREN by *Thor Hall*
FRIEDRICH SCHLEIERMACHER by *C. W. Christian*
HANS KÜNG by *John Kiwiet*
IAN T. RAMSEY by *William Williamson*
CARL F. H. HENRY by *Bob E. Patterson*
PAUL TILLICH by *John Newport*

*Makers of the Modern Theological Mind*

**Bob E. Patterson, Editor**

# WOLFHART PANNENBERG

Don H. Olive

HENDRICKSON
PUBLISHERS
PEABODY, MASSACHUSETTS 01961-3473

3606570016571

WOLFHART PANNENBERG

Copyright © 1973
Hendrickson Publishers, Inc.
P.O. Box 3473
Peabody, Massachusetts 01961–3473
All rights reserved.
Printed in the United States of America

ISBN 0–943575–68–0

**Library of Congress Cataloging-in-Publication Data**

Olive, Don H.
    Wolfhart Pannenberg / by Don H. Olive.
      p.  cm.
    Reprint. Originally published: Waco, Tex.: Word Books,
c1973. (Makers of the modern theological mind).
    Includes bibliographical references.
    ISBN 0–943575–68–0
    1. Pannenberg, Wolfhart, 1928–    I. Title. II. Series:
Makers of the modern theological mind.
[BX4827.P3044  1991]
230'.044'092–dc20                         90–28710
                                           CIP

*To the memory of*

*J. P. Olive*

28670

# Contents

# Editor's Preface

Who are the thinkers that have shaped Christian theology in our time? This series tries to answer that question by providing a reliable guide to the ideas of the men who have significantly charted the theological seas of our century. In the current revival of theology, these books will give a new generation the opportunity to be exposed to significant minds. They are not meant, however, to be a substitute for a careful study of the original works of these makers of the modern theological mind.

This series is not for the lazy. Each major theologian is examined carefully and critically—his life, his theological method, his most germinal ideas, his weaknesses as a thinker, his place in the theological spectrum, and his chief contribution to the climate of theology today. The books are written with the assumption that laymen will read them and enter into the theological dialogue that is so necessary to the church as a whole. At the same time they are carefully enough designed to give assurance to a Ph.D. student in theology preparing for his preliminary exams.

Each author in the series is a professional scholar and theologian in his own right. All are specialists on, and in

some cases have studied with, the theologians about whom
they write. Welcome to the series.

BOB E. PATTERSON, Editor
*Baylor University*

# Preface

The intent of this book is to introduce the reader to the thought of Wolfhart Pannenberg, an innovative and provocative German theologian. As Pannenberg continues to write and as more of his works are translated, the lay American reader will be provided the opportunity of entering into theological dialogue with a most original Christian thinker. It is the purpose of this book to encourage and, if possible, stimulate this dialogue by providing the reader with an orientation to a highly complex and sophisticated theology. Although this work is intended primarily for the lay reader, it is hoped that the more advanced student will also find it useful. To this end, a fairly extensive bibliography and notes are included.

I have devoted the first chapter to introducing Pannenberg to the reader. Central to this introduction is a discussion of those thinkers—some familiar and some not so familiar—who have influenced Pannenberg. As will be seen, Pannenberg incorporates many diverse strains of thought into his own original work. The second chapter is devoted to the presentation of some of the central points of Pannenberg's theology. This presentation is certainly not exhaustive of Pannenberg's various ideas nor even indicative of his wide range of interest. It is, however, representative of his thought at the present and will, I hope, provide an entrance into his distinctive thought. The third chapter relates Pannenberg's theology to some of the central currents in contemporary theology. Finally, in the last chapter some critique of Pannenberg's characteristic emphases is offered.

I wish to acknowledge my indebtedness to Professor Pannenberg for his willingness to share his own understanding of the men and ideas which have been most influential in his development. His suggestions aided immeasurably in putting together the first chapter. Special thanks are also due my friend and colleague, J. Ivyloy Bishop, who encouraged the undertaking of this work and contributed to its completion by his interest. I also thank Bob E. Patterson for several suggestions, some of which I have incorporated to the distinct advantage of this work. Finally, I happily acknowledge the contributions of my wife, who endured the fall of 1969 and the winter of 1970, when the majority of this work was done.

DON H. OLIVE

# I. The Intellectual World of Pannenberg

The world of Wolfhart Pannenberg is a rational world. It is a world presided over by a self-conscious, full-fledged commitment to reason. Whatever understanding of the life and development of the thought of Pannenberg we may hope to come to is dependent upon the proper weight being attached to this particular commitment. To underestimate this element in Pannenberg is to miss the passion that moves the man and the theologian. For with Pannenberg theology is neither avocation nor specialty but a way of life and the breath of life.

Pannenberg's life style is thoroughly impregnated with a driving determination to discriminate rationally and through this discrimination to understand the nature and structure of reality. He sets for himself no small task and abides no labor which undertakes too little. The thesis which dominates his work is as old as Plato and has been a driving force in philosophical writings as diverse as those of Hegel of Germany and Josiah Royce of the United States. Simply stated this thesis affirms that all that is real is rational. And since the real is rational, Pannenberg's commitment involves

him in the bold business of explaining the whole world of
common experience. The extent of this task is certainly a
telling indicator of the scope and ambition of Pannenberg's
most intensive efforts to date.

## THE THEOLOGICAL SETTING

Pannenberg's conviction that life is reasonable and ultimately understandable is the motive force in his turning away
from many of the more popular modes of theological thinking. Too often theology has been content with a plurality—
for reasons which will be analyzed later—which offends the
underlying rationale of a relentlessly intellectual man.
Pannenberg is intent upon restoring the unity of a whole
world in which Christian theology can take its larger and
proper place in the community of human life.[1] When contemporary theology has sought to ghettoize itself through emphasis upon a faith which is self-authenticating and a history
which is insulated from the normal concourse of events,
Pannenberg has been intent upon a rational theology which
can be part and parcel of the whole of human experience. To
this end Pannenberg is committed to a "theology of reason"
defined as an "eschatologically oriented ontology." [2]

Theology must be a reinsertion of intellectual effort into
a world from which theology has made an abject abdication
—a reinsertion precisely at the point at which the Christian
community has an intellectual responsibility to this world.
Theology must confess the peculiar nature of reality, the
reality of the end made known in Jesus. Here theology serves
rather than avoids the human community.

At the risk of overstating the contrast between Pannenberg
and another form of contemporary theology, it is evident that
Pannenberg's rational view of the world has little place for

those modes of thinking which are anxiously concerned with the extremities of life. The often quoted couplet from William Butler Yeats is the epitome of this mental set:

> Things fall apart; the center cannot hold;
> Mere anarchy is loosed upon the world.[3]

Here is proclaimed a world presided over by harsh conflicts and ultimate pessimism. Pannenberg sees no necessity in the modern mental landscape for "the center" which "cannot hold," for the dissolution of life itself. Whatever the absurdities of the human situation, the center does hold, precisely because God has revealed the structure of all reality in his self-revelation through Jesus Christ. In him is the anticipated end by which all reality hangs together. Just what this signifies will be dealt with later.

Here it is sufficient to note that Pannenberg's commitment to reason will not allow him an escape into either transcendentalism or fragmentationalism. Reality holds together in the hard reality of Jesus and opens to the perceptive and willing mind a rational understanding that is unified in and through Jesus. If "mere anarchy is loosed upon the world," it is only because of a type of irrational non-faith that refuses to see in Jesus Christ the center of all things. Reality is found in Jesus, and the man committed to a reasonable understanding can find it.

## PANNENBERG: THE MAN

Pannenberg's singular commitment to reason must not be taken in such fashion as to indicate a man lacking in humanity. Too often rationality is mistaken for a sort of disinterestedness concerning life. Pannenberg is not a man content to think and work solely within the dimensions of the academic community. The empirical demands of reason itself have pressed him into a wide-ranging and intensive examination of the many disciplines of life. The concerns of history, archaeology, sociology, psychology, and even politics have each been a part of Pannenberg's life. He is well aware that he lives in a world in which he cannot afford to shut himself off from the broadest possible range of experience. Consequently, Pannenberg has exposed himself to many worlds of thought and activity.

An example of Pannenberg's wide-ranging practical interest is his openness toward the idea of revolution. He responded sympathetically to the 1968 student revolutions at various campuses throughout the world—Berkeley, Columbia, Paris, Madrid, and Munich, to name a few. Any reservations Pannenberg may have had about these activities were based more on failure to live up to revolutionary theory than upon any basic disagreement.[4] Another example of Pannenberg's practical interest is his active role in party politics. Upon occasion he has been among those professors calling for accommodation with East Germany with regard to the settlement of border lines and other disputed questions. These positions have earned him the title of "liberal activist" in the German academic community, and are enough to dispel any idea of Pannenberg as an intellectual recluse. His life style is that of a vigorous, seeking human being.

Whatever his activity, however, Pannenberg is primarily an intellectual; that is, he is first and foremost a man dominated by intellectual concerns. Even his pilgrimage to Christianity has been intellectually oriented, coming more from rational reflection than from a conversion experience or Christian nurture.[5] Since he is so preeminently a rational man, it is to be expected that the influences responsible for shaping his thought and directing his personal development have come primarily from contact with other minds. As important as his personal biography may be, the decisive influences on Pannenberg have been those incisive minds with whom he has had contact. Before moving on to an examination of these influences, however, a presentation of some of the basic circumstances of Pannenberg's life will certainly do nothing to confuse our understanding.

Pannenberg was born in 1928, almost exactly midway between the two great European wars of the present century. His father was a typical, middle-class, German civil servant. From all accounts, his home did not profess a devotional type of Christianity. Pannenberg received the usual education available for a gifted child, even though he grew up in the midst of the Great Depression. Although he was too young to feel the full impact of nazism, Pannenberg retains a distinct impression of the last few sad days of the Third Reich. Along with a multitude of other German youths, he was pressed into the last desperate effort to defend Germany. Understandably, this has left him with a vivid impression of nazism and a resultant caution concerning society in general and German society in particular.

Pannenberg's contact with the great minds of Germany began with his entrance into the university system in the late 1940s. In 1950 at Basel, Pannenberg was strongly influenced by Karl Barth, the noted Swiss theologian. The next year he moved to Heidelberg University where his most important years as a student were spent. His philosophical training had begun under Nicolai Hartmann at Göttingen in 1948–49, continued under Karl Jaspers at Basel, and focused particularly upon the philosophy of history under Karl Löwith at Heidelberg from 1951 to 1953. Pannenberg also studied under such notable German scholars as Hans von Campenhausen, Heinrich Vogel, Peter Brunner, Edmund Schlink, and Gerhard von Rad.

Pannenberg's scholarly publication began in 1954 with a dissertation entitled *Duns Scotus' Doctrine of Predestination.*[6] Since then he has written prolifically for various journals, and has written and edited several books. Most of his works have now been translated into English. He was for several years Professor of Systematic Theology at the University of Mainz, moving in 1968 to the same position at the University of Munich.

Pannenberg's contact with the United States has been fairly extensive, if not always fortunate. He has lectured at Harvard, Yale, the University of Chicago, and the School of Theology at Claremont, California. Regrettably, some of Pannenberg's contacts here produced a mismatch of minds, such that after the lectures at the University of Chicago, Harvard, and the School of Theology at Claremont his "impact" was characterized as "something short of over-whelming."[7] Nevertheless, his lectures here and the American contact with his thought have served to make Pannenberg one of the better known younger German theologians. He has been popularly feted by *Time* and *Newsweek* and has been briefly courted by *Christianity Today.* It will be interesting to see how Pannenberg's relationship with the United States continues to develop.

## INTELLECTUAL DEVELOPMENT

As has been noted, the most decisive elements in the make-up of Pannenberg's thought derive from the various minds with which he has dialogued. He credits three men with very special significance in the formation of his thought—Gerhard von Rad, Hans von Campenhausen, and Karl Löwith.[8]

*The Influence of von Rad*

The impact of Gerhard von Rad, the well-known German Old Testament scholar, on theology has been striking. The influence on Pannenberg is no less exceptional. Von Rad's thesis that theology is ultimately an interpretation of history has been a most important contribution to Pannenberg's thought. Von Rad contends that theology is primarily concerned with the Old Testament statements—in confessional or creedal form—of a continuing divine activity in history. The study of these creeds in their original form, together with the later elaborations or meditations upon them, is the sole proper subject matter of theological effort.

Von Rad sees an explicit difference between the general historical task and the more restricted task of Old Testament theology. Historical research examines the spiritual and religious world of Israel and her world of faith through a conscious and diligent study of Israel's documents. The task of theology, on the other hand, is concerned with "simply Israel's own explicit assertions about Yahweh." [9] Since these explicit assertions are assertions about Yahweh's acts in Israel's history, it must be taken that in principle Israel's faith is grounded in a theology of history. Israel saw herself shaped and formed by historical acts interpreted as the hand of Yahweh at work.

Through these emphases and von Rad's general theological approach, Pannenberg was introduced to much that is determinative for his thought. From von Rad Pannenberg receives the conviction that the Old Testament is indispensable to theological thought. Much of Pannenberg's work is connected with New Testament studies, but it is from an Old Testament perspective that Pannenberg finds the New Testament intelligible at all. In the deepest sense possible, the New Testament is dependent upon the Old, so much so that without the Old the New would have no meaning.

Von Rad also bequeathes to Pannenberg the idea that history is an indispensable element of human life. Until von Rad, most theologies of the Old Testament were singularly lacking in this basic understanding. Most were concerned to present some kind of cross section through the world of ancient Israelic thought. From these cross sections, then, were drawn out those doctrines that to each theologian seemed most basic for his purposes. In contrast, von Rad provides a theological understanding which is firmly grounded in the historical element of the Old Testament. Pannenberg maintains this emphasis in his own thought.

Another concept for which Pannenberg is in debt to von Rad is that of the relation of the biblical God to history. Von Rad insists that Yahweh's revelation is "bound to time and hour." [10] Whatever else may be known of Yahweh, it must be affirmed that he is known primarily through his relationship with the events of Israel's history as reported in her confessions of faith. In light of this concept Pannenberg's theological understanding is firmly committed to revelation in "time and hour" events.

These are important areas in which Pannenberg agrees with and is dependent upon von Rad. There is, however, at least one area of profound disagreement. Von Rad is primarily interested in the God who acts in the history of Israel as reported in the creeds, whereas Pannenberg is more interested in the totality of history. Von Rad insists that the subject matter of an Old Testament theology can never be the "systematically ordered 'world of the faith' of Israel" and even less "the 'history' of this world of faith." [11] Old Testament theology has as its subject matter only the confessed history of Israel.

This limiting of theology to the history of Israel is for Pannenberg an unsatisfactory by-pass of the actual stuff of history—the events upon which the confessions were based. Critical history, a synonym for universal or nonconfessional history, is relegated by von Rad to the nontheological realm of modern critical historical scholarship. The nature of the events as events remains unknown and uninteresting to the theologian. In the final analysis Pannenberg's rationality cannot accept this limiting to the confessed history of Israel. Theology must speak in and of universal history.

## The Influence of von Campenhausen

Another who has profoundly influenced Pannenberg is Hans von Campenhausen, professor and theologian at Heidelberg University. Von Campenhausen's influence is closely allied with the theological situation in postwar Germany, and especially as it came into focus at Heidelberg University. By the time Pannenberg moved to Heidelberg, the mainstream of postwar German theological reconstruction had already begun. The reconstruction, coming after the theological drought of the war years, resulted in an atmosphere of heated excitement generated by such men as von Campenhausen, von Rad, Schlink, Löwith, and others. The excitement became so intense that there was "standing room only" space in the university library and theological seminary.

A part of this quickening was generated by von Campenhausen's rectoral address at the reopening of the University.[12] Entitled "Augustine and the Fall of Rome," the address sought to draw from Augustine's observations upon the fall of Rome parallels for German thinking in the ashes of World War II. Von Campenhausen contended that when Augustine and early Christianity were confronted with the end of civilization as they had known it, they challenged the world to a

critical revision of the dominant historical consciousness
rather than lead a retreat from historical reality.

Von Campenhausen maintained that just such a program
lay before a ruined Germany. Theology cannot turn over to
its pagan opponents all of history, no matter how tragic that
history may appear to be. Von Campenhausen said, "One
must speak to the issues, and the religious apology thus becomes a critical revision of the dominant historic consciousness, a struggle for the proper possession of one's own past
and of political history as a whole." [13] This bold statement
of the place and scope of a reconstructed theological endeavor
in the teeth of a predominantly negative historical situation
served as a catalyst for revived theological thought.

The call for a revised historic consciousness, for the possession of political history as a whole, not only challenged the
consciousness of history but also reached deep into the historical disciplines. This was a call for rethinking historical
criticism, the philosophy of history, and scriptural exegesis.
Within the context of this rethinking, Pannenberg was first
introduced to the principles of historical criticism. A man
firmly involved in history itself could not regard the principles of historical criticism as peripheral to life. Whatever
the problems of historical criticism, they were problems that
demanded treatment. This much Pannenberg learned from
von Campenhausen.

The possession of political history as a whole advocated
by von Campenhausen aroused in Pannenberg a suspicious
attitude toward what he regards as an unnatural hiatus
between ordinary history and special histories of salvation.
More will be said in a later chapter about Pannenberg's
specific formulations concerning history as a whole. Here
it is necessary to remember that the theologian is not to be
allowed a retreat from the actualities of ordinary history.

The possession of political history and one's own past does not allow the luxury of a secure sacred history where there is a minimum of involvement with the actual course of history —its wars, tragedies, and griefs.

From von Campenhausen, Pannenberg also received a hermeneutical awareness. When there is a self-conscious awareness of historical change, man realizes he no longer lives in the biblical age nor, for that matter, in the age of Augustine, Aquinas, or Luther. The relationship to the Bible can never again be explained sufficiently in terms of an exegesis of texts. Only a full awareness of the differences and connections of historical epochs will allow the interpreter to relate himself rightly to the Bible. The end result of this awareness is a recognition of the difference between the exegesis of a text and the text's evaluation by the historian. To confuse the two is to falsify the historic consciousness of man. Pannenberg accepts this differentiation as a valid methodological principle.

## The Influence of Karl Löwith

The third man of formative influence upon Pannenberg is the philosopher Karl Löwith.[14] Pannenberg first came into contact with Löwith's thought by means of Löwith's lectures in the philosophy of history at Heidelberg in the early fifties.

In *Meaning in History* Löwith contends that all modern philosophies of history are dependent upon and nourished by the biblical theology of history. This dependency does not make the problem of deciphering a meaning in history from within the perspective of history itself any easier to solve. "Seen in the light of the faith that God is revealed in the historical man, Jesus Christ, the profane events before and after Christ are not a solid chain of meaningful successions but spurious happenings whose significance or insignificance is to be judged in the perspective of their possible signification of judgment and salvation." [15] Thus since Christ was but the beginning of an end of a history now redeemed and "dismantled," Christians cannot be a historical people. Modern man's transformation of eschatology into a religious concept of progress is symptomatic of the radical dissolution of meaning in history under the impact of Christ. Ultimately, "a 'Christian history' is non-sense." [16] Löwith contends that redemptive history is a suprahistory which excludes any theology of history such as Augustine's, precisely because a theology of history tends to include all events.

Pannenberg's debt to Löwith derives from Löwith's basic assumption that all modern philosophy of history is nourished by the biblical theology of history.[17] Pannenberg, however, does not think it necessary to conclude with Löwith that the philosophy of history is symptomatic of a modern overrating of history. He turns Löwith's argument around in an affirmative way by emphasizing that the error of modern historical thinking lies not in the constructing of a philosophy of history but rather in "the fact that since the Enlightenment, since Vico and Voltaire, man has been exalted to the place of God as the one who bears history." [18]

The deterioration of modern philosophy of history in the West does not necessarily imply a deviation from its origin in the Christian understanding of history. Pannenberg rescues the discipline of the philosophy of history by attributing deviations to man's attempt to be God. When taken positively, the Jewish-Christian understanding of history is still the presupposition and origin of the Western consciousness of historical reality.

Although von Rad, von Campenhausen, and Löwith are the men who have been most influential in Pannenberg's development, two other men deserve special note. Edmund

Schlink, with whom Pannenberg took his doctoral degree at Heidelberg, impressed upon Pannenberg the importance of the ecumenical problem and influenced his interest in the formal problems of theological statements.[19] And from Karl Jaspers Pannenberg received an awareness of the impossibility of a closed system in the modern intellectual situation where authoritarian structures have collapsed.[20]

## THEOLOGICAL BACKGROUNDS

Like all other theologians, Pannenberg works out of some very definite theological backgrounds against which his thought stands out. There are at least three of these.

### The Barthian Background

Pannenberg was a student of Barth at Basel and to this time admits to being a "rather peculiar Barthian."[21] Although much of Pannenberg's relationship to Barth is primarily that of a reaction against, he rightly realizes that he and all other theologians work within a setting that is profoundly in debt to Barth. A theologian cannot disregard this giant of theology; he can only work through him.

Pannenberg owes much to Barth, particularly to the impact of his commitment and responsibility to the continuing traditions of Christian thought.[22] More immediate, however, is the debt owed to Barth for the insight concerning revelation—an insight given to theology as a whole. It is Barth who sees best of all that theology must strictly be viewed as a function of revelation. The very nature of revelation demands as much.

Revelation is revelation precisely and only because it is the *self-revelation* of God. Revelation can never be some set of arcane truths about God—truths guaranteed by some doc-

trine of the inspiration of the Bible. The Enlightenment effectively challenged this concept when it demonstrated the
historicity of the Bible. Thus for Barth revelation must be
the self-disclosure of God and as such is the ground for
theology. However much various theologies differ from
Barth's understanding of the content of revelation, few if
any are willing to nullify the understanding that revelation
is somehow the self-presentation of God. This is Barth's
legacy to modern theology.

   Closely allied with this concept of revelation is Barth's
concentration upon the person of Jesus Christ. Since God's
revelation is self-revelation, Christ must be the truly unique
revelation. Pannenberg comments that "those rejecting
Barth's conception that revelation in Christ is a truly unique
one have obviously not properly considered that the uniqueness of revelation is already implied in the context of
'self-revelation.' " [23] Without doubt it is from Barth that Pannenberg has learned the centrality of Jesus Christ in any theological enterprise.

   Beyond these points, however, Pannenberg finds it necessary to part company with Barth. Pannenberg's interest in
philosophy and the absence of philosophical precision in
Barth's thought make it impossible for him to be a strict
Barthian. For Barth the self-revelation of God only comes to
man in veiled form, since revelation necessarily implies
a veiling. [24] Revelation is to be understood only in the sphere
of God's grace delineated totally at the will and discretion of
God. Man's understanding of this revelation is necessarily
limited by man's finitude. Here Barth falls back upon the
Calvinistic axiom that the finite is not capable of the infinite. [25]
The primary cognitive aspect of revelation must always remain with God.

   Pannenberg strongly disagrees. The primary cognitive aspect of revelation must lie with man, or it is not revelation. Revelation is the self-disclosure of God, but in order to be revelation it must not lie outside the normal sphere of man's potential understanding. This basic disagreement with Barth led Pannenberg to pursue the development of his theological thought along more philosophical lines, and he turned to a more intense critical historical study than Barth ever accomplished. In addition Pannenberg involved himself seriously in general, nontheological thought in a way that Barth did not consider necessary. But even these differences are emphases which have arisen out of intimate contact with Barth.

## The Hegelian Background

Although Pannenberg reports that he did not read Hegel until 1956–57 in conjunction with a course he taught on "Protestant Theology in the Nineteenth Century," he was immediately impressed with Hegel's high level of intellectual sophistication in the presentation of highly complex philosophical problems. This impression has had more lasting impact upon Pannenberg than Hegel's actual solution to the complex problems.

Pannenberg's adaptation of Hegel's view of universal history as the self-disclosure of God is so central to his thought and so decisive for his position that he is often accused of merely restating Hegel. Although Hegelian idealism is not currently in fashion, Pannenberg has not for that reason alone been willing to relinquish this central concept. With tongue in cheek Pannenberg reminds us that Barth's concept of revelation as the self-revelation of God came from Hegel indirectly through the Hegelian, Philipp Marheineke. And this is no reason at all to reject the insight. Pannenberg states: "We should also remember that to locate a theological thought in German idealism is not automatically to condemn it."[26] And, of course, Pannenberg is correct.

Pannenberg makes full use of Hegel, but by no means is he merely reformulating him. Pannenberg is at full liberty to make interpretations and changes within the framework of his own understanding. This he does and yet retains the understanding that Christianity rests upon the general process of history—a process which is the full disclosure of God. History is the self-revelation of God. In history God makes himself known. Pannenberg quotes Marheineke as saying, "It is not through the human spirit as such that God is revealed, but through himself and then to the human spirit."[27] To Pannenberg this is too valuable a concept to be relinquished for the sake of placating modern antiidealism.

## The Team Theology Background

One further background element for Pannenberg's thought deserves extensive mention. It is by nature more general and consequently more subtle and difficult to delineate. It arises out of Pannenberg's participation in a small group of men who first met while graduate students at Heidelberg. This group later became known—against Pannenberg's wishes—as the Pannenberg circle.

The circle only slowly crystallized and became evident in the 1950s through the publication of the various members' dissertations and *Habilitationsschriften*.[28] The works of the circle ranged from intense exegetical studies of Scripture to practical matters of pastoral counseling. Underlying this general diversity, however, was a central theme which became explicit with the publication in 1959 of Pannenberg's programmatic essay entitled "Redemptive Event and History."[29] The lead sentence of this essay set forth the unifying concept: "History is the most comprehensive horizon of Christian theology." [30]

The Pannenberg circle has been described as a new movement which was "the first to emerge from the German generation that was born well after World War I had passed, was raised in the throes of the Third Reich, World War II, and the collapse of 1945, and has reached maturity in the *Bundesrepublik.*" [31] Pannenberg specifically credits Martin Elze, Klaus Koch, Rolf Rendtorff, Dietrich Rossler, and Ulrich Wilkens as members of the circle and men who profoundly influenced him through "continuing conversation." Although there is some disagreement as to the actual extent of the circle, there is little doubt as to its originality and creativity. [32]

The central motif of the circle set it apart from other prominent schools of theology. The statement that history is the most comprehensive horizon of Christian theology presupposes a need for critical historical study of Scripture in a way that neoorthodoxy has never affirmed. The Bible must be totally immersed in the stuff of history. On the other hand, the circle's motif assumes an involvement of Christian theology with the disciplines common to man's life to a degree that the existential theology of the Bultmannians has not attained. Theology must not be allowed to retreat into a subjective realm where it is separated from the vigorous province of intellectual activity. It must remain in the world of man's history.

The theological program of the circle provided as much, if not more, of the background of Pannenberg's thought as did its theological formulations. This program was in direct opposition to two tendencies of contemporary theology—the tendency toward fragmenting the theological endeavor into isolated specialties and the tendency toward ghettoizing theol-

ogy into a monastic exercise cut off from practical understanding. The Pannenberg circle intended by its program of
theological activity constructively to overcome these tendencies.

The methodological novelty of "team theology" has been
an attempt at healing the fractures which occur when theology
shrinks from the universality of its intellectual task. A circle of specialists, sharing the common elements of their specialties, provides a comprehensiveness normally impossible
for any one man. Within the framework of mutual theological
cooperation, Pannenberg participated fully in this impulse
toward comprehensiveness.

## CONCLUSION

In concluding this section, one other man deserves mention,
not because he has significantly affected Pannenberg but
rather because it is sometimes mistakenly assumed that he
has. Although there is a surprising convergence of the
thoughts of Pannenberg and Ernst Bloch, a German philosopher, much of Pannenberg's thought had already taken
shape by the time he read Bloch seriously in 1963.[33] At
the time, Pannenberg's christology was already essentially
complete, and his concept of "anticipation" as the central
category of chistology had already been delineated in *Revelation as History*.[34] Thus whatever similarities may exist,
Pannenberg's concept and terminology cannot be directly attributed to a dependence upon Bloch.

These then are some of the more evident men and factors
that have influenced Pannenberg up to the present. We must
not forget, however, that no man's thought is explained as
the sum of the influences brought to bear upon his thinking.
Pannenberg has combined and selected from the emphases

communicated to him from a rich background to produce a creative and fresh mentality on the theological scene. Since he is still a young man, his thought may very well continue to develop. But as it does so, it can reasonably be expected to develop along the lines of the fertile concepts suggested already in Pannenberg's past.

# II. Pannenberg
## at Work

In a discussion of Pannenberg's theological position, two problems immediately present themselves. The first problem arises out of the fact that Pannenberg is still in the process of developing, clarifying, and systematizing his thought. Likely it will be some time before he is ready to give us a comprehensive theological statement in systematic form, complete with methodological prolegomenon—indeed he may never see fit to do so. Consequently, any attempt to present his thought in systematic form will at this juncture be somewhat premature and is bound to seem somewhat stilted, if not moribund. Since there are certain motifs rather thoroughly treated by Pannenberg, however, an approach to his thought that presents these motifs in relation to one another is probably the best suited to the situation. This is the approach that will be used here.

The second problem confronted in discussing Pannenberg's theology is his creativity. There is always a possibility of overemphasizing this aspect in any writer; and yet, the statement that "Pannenberg's work is . . . the most creative

that is now being done in theology" has much to commend it.[1]
True creativity does not place a premium upon complexity,
neither does it necessarily involve something so novel as to
make analysis impossible. Certainly this is the case with
Pannenberg; and yet his creativity does pose a problem. It
is difficult to reverse fields and long-established mind patterns. This is precisely what Pannenberg is asking his reader
to do, and thereby he is posing a difficulty for those of us
theologically trained to some form of a Barthian or Bultmannian tradition. This, of course, says more about the interpreter than it does about Pannenberg. Nevertheless, it is a
factor when coming to grips with Pannenberg's theological
formulations. His creativity—his questioning of contemporary theological modes—is a challenge, and precisely for
that reason a difficulty.

Basic to an understanding of Pannenberg's theology is an
appreciation of his commitment to a reasonable theological
stance. This reasonableness, though often strange to present
theological efforts, is nevertheless part and parcel of that
which Pannenberg considers the best in modern man. The
Christian faith cannot abandon itself to some small corner
of intellectual endeavor and hope to be relevant to life and to
itself—even less can it abandon its true role in a time when
there is a call for a comprehensive approach to life. Modern
man will no longer willingly put on blinders in order to think
theologically; neither can the Christian God survive as a
sort of truncated, provincial deity who is limited to some
religious dimension of life.

The bifurcation of life into religious and nonreligious
zones will no longer suffice as a description of man's duty
before God. If the Christian intellectual effort is to survive,
God must be affirmed to be what he affirms himself to be

—creator and Lord of life. This theological affirmation is demanded by Christian rationality. Pannenberg intends to undergo the discipline required to meet this demand.

To thrust Christian theology out into the mainstream of human activity in this way is to run headlong into the perennial problem of the philosophy-theology relationship. A considerable amount of Pannenberg's efforts is expended in dealing with topics around which this problem revolves. And it is to this problem that we come first in examining Pannenberg's thought.

## THE UNIVERSAL SCIENCE

In defining the proper relationship between philosophy and theology, Pannenberg makes the unhesitating claim that theology is a universal science. Such an affirmation immediately raises the question of how theology is to be considered a science at the same level as the other sciences. This question is particularly urgent when the subject matter proper to the theological science is today suspected of being an illusion.[2]

Pannenberg accuses many theologians of seeking to avoid this attack by advocating an understanding of God which is accessible only to individual experience or to a decision of faith—neither of which can be expressed in an objective statement. For Pannenberg this is little more than an ill-advised and ill-disguised retreat. Theology can just as validly take the opposite tack and "dare a breakthrough into the universal consciousness of truth."[3] To do so is, of course, to recall the periods of history when Christian theology was considered the only true philosophy. This is precisely what Pannenberg intends. If theology is allowed to withdraw and become only a science among other sciences, it has already violated its own subject matter, the universal, monotheistic

God. Pannenberg writes: "A conception of reality in relation to God, such that it cannot be understood at all without God, belongs to the task of theology. And that constitutes its universality." [4]

Pannenberg contends that the withdrawal of theology from its proper universality is explained by the "scripture-principle" or "scripture-positivism" of Protestant theology. Protestant theology has again and again sought to limit itself to the interpretation of Scripture. But precisely by such an act theology is shut off from the mainstream of intellectual effort, and its genius of universality is destroyed.

In the Enlightenment the other sciences changed when the scientist no longer felt bound to agree with the Bible; but theology, by becoming a positive science of Scripture interpretation, refused any important changes. Subsequently, the differences between theology and secular science mounted, until a decision between a static theological science and a dynamic secular science became necessary. Faced with this decision, more and more modern men chose secular science. Theology became peripheral and surrendered its universality. Bound to "scripture-positivism," theology then performed its own narrow task to the detriment of the concept of God proper to it.

Pannenberg intends to reverse this improper surrender of theological universality. But when this reversal is made, there remains little room for a second universal science such as philosophy. Although Pannenberg does not deal directly with this concern, he does ask the question: "Can there really be more than one universal science?" To this question he answers, "It is doubtful!" Theology must be the one universal science and take upon itself a universal scope of activity. No longer can it exclude certain nonreligious features, certain scientific areas of life, from the sphere of its activity.

It cannot withdraw from the most overarching categories of reality. To be a universal science means it must be able to supply an idea of reality such that every experience of life is understandable within its framework. It must supply cognitive significance to every dimension of human experience. Theology must assume this bold, comprehensive task, unless it is willing to be guilty itself of disobedience against the first commandment.[5]

As a universal science, theology is reelevated to the place of "queen of the sciences," although certainly not in the earlier sense of dictator. Theology is not to impose either subject matter or methodology upon the other sciences. It does not need to do so if it will free itself from the demands of a "scripture-positivism" in which the outcome of scientific discovery is already dictated by a literal interpretation of the Scripture. Theology's proper task is to provide the ground upon which all other disciplines can become fully what they can be. The sciences all benefit as individual disciplines precisely because each is provided with the valid ontological ground—the creator, sustainer God. Theology serves as the comprehensive discipline because its subject matter is God.

## FAITH AND REASON

Closely aligned with the concept of a universal science is the insertion of faith into the public arena. Since theology is a public affair, faith cannot be allowed a retreat into a private world of personal experience. It cannot be a special way of knowing, immune to the open demands of human rationality. To make faith such is to fragment truth into that which is true according to faith and that which is true according to reason. Faith becomes the way of knowing the truth of private revelation; science becomes the means into the public truth of nature, history, or philosophy.

Such a scheme denies the oneness of truth and for Pannenberg raises grave questions concerning this concept. Pannenberg affirms that "for much too long a time faith has been misunderstood to be subjectivity's fortress into which Christianity could retreat from the attacks of scientific knowledge." [6] This retreat into pious subjectivity can only lead in today's world to the destruction of any consciousness of the truth of the Christian faith. Any attempt at the bifurcation of truth is in "danger of distorting the historical revelation into a gnostic knowledge of secrets." [7]

Since truth is one, faith must be understood in such a way as to preserve this oneness. "Theology," says Pannenberg, "has no reason or excuse to cheapen the character and value of a truth that is open to general reasonableness." [8] Thus in order for truth to remain open to general reasonableness, faith must have primarily to do with what Jesus was—that is, with the activity and fate of Jesus in the past. Stated another way, faith has to do with the historical truth that is open to all historical investigation.

The events of Jesus' fate must be the logical presupposition of faith and not vice versa. Without a well-founded historical knowledge, "faith would be blind gullibility, credulity, or even superstition." [9] Faith must have the conviction that its foundation is true—a conviction the fate of Jesus carries to the reasonable eyes of any who will see. The Holy Spirit is not "an additional condition without which the event of Christ could not be known as revelation," but rather the "gift received by means of faith." [10] It is a complete misunderstanding of faith to conceive of it as a verifying principle applied to God's self-revelation in universal history. It is reason's task to verify that which is openly given to all.

At this point Pannenberg is careful to avoid two possible misconceptions. First, for him to say that the knowledge of revelation is supplied apart from supernatural devices is not to say that man only confirms what he already knows through the force of his own intellect. Even though the Holy Spirit does not justify man's faith through a special illumination, "no one comes to the knowledge of God by his own reason or strength." [11] The force of the knowledge of revelation is resident within the events and the report of these events, not within man himself.

Thus man's reason by which he grasps the events of revelation must itself be transformed, as the events of revelation have the power to do. The fact that many men—perhaps even the majority of men—do not see the facts as they naturally emerge from the events of revelation should in no way be interpreted to mean that reason must be supplemented by other means of knowing. Rather it means only that men must better "use their reason in order to see correctly." [12] Reason must be transformed, not transmuted or displaced. And the events of revelation have the power to transform it.

The second misconception to be avoided is that of saying "that faith is made superfluous by the knowledge of God's revelation in the events that demonstrate his deity." [13] As long as faith is the instrument by which past events receive meaning and significance, or as long as faith is considered a function of the relationship between the believer and the present Christ, Pannenberg's approach will indeed appear to displace faith by knowledge. However, it is only the faulty connection of faith to either the past or present that produces this conclusion. The past and the present are the domains of reason; faith is by its nature connected with the future.

Faith has to do with the future, for therein lies the primary essence of trust. Trust is the risk of life and future upon that which has presented itself as trustworthy. In order not to be blissful gullibility, faith must be grounded upon the reasonable events that point toward the future which either justifies or disappoints. Faith is still the risk taken on the "fact of God's having been revealed in the fate of Jesus." Thus faith is not arrived at blindly but "by means of an event that can be appropriated as something that can be considered reliable." [14]

Faith then involves the Christian not so much in a past series of events as in an open-ended future that is set upon the facts of God's revelation in universal history. Through faith men are called toward the future that is opened by the natural significance of the events of the activity and fate of Jesus. In this way only the knowledge of God's revelation can be the foundation of faith. And yet it must be emphasized "that it is not knowledge, but the resulting faith in God that secures participation in salvation." [15]

Although faith is primary for salvation, reason provides the foundation for that faith. That is to say, reason is the logical presupposition of faith. The self-revelation of God in the event of Jesus presents a natural understanding in terms of this event. This understanding provides the trustworthy foundation from which faith proceeds.

Throughout the discussion of theology as a universal science and of faith and reason as complementary functions of the Christian understanding, it is evident that Pannenberg is intent upon providing a way of thought that is characterized first and foremost by unity, consistency, and coherence. For Pannenberg there is one reality, consisting of one history made known to man through the events of that history. This reality is without special conditions, it is without different ways of knowing, and it is without fragmentation. It is in fact God's self-revelation to man.

## REALITY AS HISTORY

The Pannenberg circle's most complete and characteristic expression is found in the book entitled *Offenbarung als Geschichte*. This work has been translated into English under the title *Revelation as History*. The title of this cooperative effort provides two crucial concepts around which Pannenberg's direct theological thinking revolves. In one fashion or another much of his thought harks back to the foundational work presented in this study. The problem then is to discern in what sense Pannenberg can speak of revelation as history.[16]

An entrance into this problem is provided by Pannenberg's intense study of the hermeneutical question—the question of how modern man is to interpret and understand the Bible.[17] Conscious of the questions presented by the philosophy of history, Pannenberg approaches modern hermeneutics via a discussion of the history of the discipline and an examination of the inadequacies of present hermeneutical schemes. A brief survey of this approach will be valuable.

Prior to and including Luther, "the verbal sense of the Scriptures was still identical with their historical content." The chief question for theology was the question of authority rather than the more formal hermeneutical question. But with the dissolution of this view under the impact of the development of historical research, the historical content of Scripture was separated from the picture of that content given by the writers. In addition to an awareness of this separation, there has also arisen an awareness of the "historical distance between every possible theology today and the early Christian period." [18]

These two related conditions actually pose the hermeneutical problem for modern man in more acute form than has been possible in any other time. Modern hermeneutics must come to grips with a twofold distance, that between the interpreter and the text and that between the text and the event. In so doing hermeneutics must deal with the problem of how a given content from the past can be repeated in a completely changed situation in the present. The question is how the distance between the past of the texts and the present of the interpreter can be bridged.

In an attempt to answer this question, Pannenberg turns to a survey of notable hermeneutical efforts—those of Schleiermacher, Dilthey, Bultmann, and Fuchs. Each one of these efforts—Schleiermacher's intuition based on common humanity, Dilthey's reconstruction of the "creative event," Bultmann's existential preunderstanding, and Fuchs' characterization of the text as address—shares a common weakness. In each case the relationship of the past and the interpreter is already established in a presupposed common element. This common element eliminates for the interpreter everything which is not already present in present experience. The common element must already be known to the interpreter. "The pre-understanding of life and the possibilities of experience," Pannenberg contends, "thus condition and limit interpretation from the outset." [19]

The only solution of the hermeneutical problem which does not participate in the foregoing limitation is one which further develops modern thought, so as to bring it again "into a more conscious connection with Christian tradition." [20] That is to say, modern thought must be expanded to incorporate

the biblical idea of universal history. As long as the interpreter foists upon the historical process some presupposed
element common to past and present, he cannot adequately
respect the differences between the times. It is Pannenberg's
contention, in contrast, that the historical understanding inherent in the concept of universal history is capable of being
expanded backwards in such a way as to eventually include
the past in the present understanding. In this way the hermeneutical differences between the past of the text and the
present of the interpreter are both respected and overcome.
They are respected in that there is no assumption of any necessarily common elements in past and present. They are
overcome in that both past and present are incorporated
within the larger framework of universal history. All this is
possible when universal history "can again be regarded as
the work of the biblical God." [21]

In setting forth his concept of understanding inherent in
the idea of universal history, Pannenberg makes extensive use
of the analysis of the process of historical understanding presented in H.-G. Gadamer's book, *Wahrheit und Methode*.[22]
Gadamer contends that historical understanding must be approached from the fact that both past and present have certain historical horizons or limits beyond which understanding
cannot go. Although the past's horizon cannot change, the
horizon of the present is capable of expansion. As the text in
question comes to be understood by the interpreter, his own
horizon is broadened to include even that which is strange and
outside his normal horizon of understanding. "In the confrontation of the interpreter with his text," says Pannenberg,
"a new, a single horizon is formed, which includes everything
which the historical consciousness contains within itself." [23]
Thus in interpretation there occurs a melting of horizons, that
is, an enlargement of the "intellectual horizon of the inter-

preter to such an extent that it can also encompass the horizon of the text to be interpreted." [24]

This approach to historical understanding presupposes that man comes to terms with the totality of life in connection with the totality of reality. Man comes to understand reality through a conscious movement toward an infinite historical horizon which is constantly enlarging and being revised by this enlargement. Pannenberg sees this idea as having its origin in the biblical concept of history and of God. He writes: "Only the almighty and yet faithful God of Israelitic tradition gave rise to an understanding of reality as a history of ever new events, in contrast to the Greek understandings of the world as an eternal order for which the novelty of events had no essential importance." [25]

The enlargement of the present's horizon has a goal of a universal horizon of history in which the understanding of reality is accomplished by the total mediation of past and present. Reality is the historical process, and man's understanding of reality is an aggregate of historical accommodation on the part of the present.

At this point it is advisable to say just a word as to how Pannenberg differentiates his thought concerning historical reality from Hegel's philosophy of the spirit. For Hegel history is subsumed under the concept of the absolute self-consciousness of philosophy. "Of world history," writes Hegel, "it may be said that it is the account of the spirit, how it works to attain the *knowledge* of what it is *in itself*." [26] The recounting of human experience is thus the way of understanding the absolute spirit. World history is the account of the spirit.

Although Pannenberg agrees with Hegel to the point that world history is the revelation of God, he feels Hegel has missed a constitutive element of reality—the finiteness of

human experience. No concept of history can be absolutized
as long as finitude is maintained as the vantage point of
thinking. Man does not know all of a history that still has a
future yet to come, and by the same token he does not know
all of God's revelation. This is the one point that "makes any
simple repetition of Hegel's system impossible." [27]

Reality as history must remain open-ended—a goal accomplished in Pannenberg's thought through the openness of history to the future. Man's history has a contingent future that
continually presses in upon the present. History is always incomplete; the present is always directed toward the future.
Man's present is always subject to an unfathomable number
of contingent events. Man does not live in the final future
"but rather is ever and again surprised by what comes upon
him from the future." [28] It is this understanding that sets
Pannenberg apart from Hegel's view of universal history.

It is to be expected that Pannenberg's concept of universal
history demands a method of historical research that is also
universal. Unless faith is based upon a historiography
available to all men, it can be little more than superstition.
The current theological tendency to ground faith in itself
Pannenberg sees as having arisen in Martin Kahler's *The
So-Called Historical Jesus and the Historic, Biblical Christ.*[29]
In this work the source of Christian theology is not to be
found in history but rather in the "content" of the preached
Christ.[30] This emphasis upon the content of proclamation
led to the easy dismissal of history, universal historiography,
and an independently grounded faith. Theology became fas-
cinated with the involution of faith upon itself.

Later, in the Barthian tradition theology becomes interested in *Heilsgeschichte*, a special kind of salvation history
in which revelation takes place in events immune to general
historical methods. Bultmann reinforces this emphasis by an-

nouncing the end of history in Christ in such a way that eschatology becomes primarily present meaning rather than future events. The theologian is not interested in the events of history at all. He is only interested in the meaning possible for present existence through the fact of Christ. Historical methodology as applied, for instance, to the resurrection has nothing to do with the existential encounter with Christ.

Thus for both Barth and Bultmann the historic Christ is radically separated from the events of Jesus' fate and activity. The result is a view of faith and history that obviates the need for historical research upon the level of a universal historiography. Pannenberg takes a most negative view of this approach. "The emancipation of historicity from history, the reversal of the relationship between the two so that history is grounded in the historicity of man—this seems to be the end of the way which began when modern man made man instead of God the one who bears history." [31]

For Pannenberg there can only be one historiography, precisely because in the final analysis there is only one history. This universal historiography is set forth in Pannenberg's *Jesus—God and Man.* It is defined by two programmatic statements—one positive, one negative. The positive historiographical condition insists that the meaning of universal history cannot be derived from one small segment of the historical fabric. The meaning of history can only be known at the end or completion of history. No absolute meaning can be ascribed to a historically differentiated reality before the completion of that reality. Man must, therefore, maintain an openness to the future.

The ability to maintain both meaning and openness is given in the resurrection of Jesus. Because the resurrection is depicted as the arrival in the present of an event proper to the future consummation, all history before this consummation has a derived meaning. This is not to say that present history is devoid of meaning altogether. It is rather to say that since Jesus' resurrection breaks through the normal categories of understanding, man must remain open to the still-to-come future of God. Thus a properly universal historiography cannot limit itself to the meaning of the present. The resurrection guarantees as much.

The negative historiographical condition derives from a criticism of the use of analogy in historical research. Analogy is a revered tool in modern historiography and works from the assumption that there is a basic similarity in all historical events.[32] Consequently, it is to be assumed that the events of the past can be understood along the same lines as the events of the present. Now, the only problem with this concept is the indiscriminate use of analogy so as to make it the criterion by which the reality or actuality of an event is determined. Such a usage oversteps the proper limits of the critical historical method. If a reported event is not analogous to what is otherwise customary or is frequently attested, this in itself is not sufficient ground for contesting that event's factuality.

Pannenberg's criticism of analogy is thus not directed against the proper use of the principle but rather against its abuse. To make the lack of analogical features as determinative for nonhistoricity as the presence of those features is for historicity is to abuse a valuable tool. The principle of analogy should remain an instrument of method and not become the final arbiter of reality.[33]

Pannenberg's historical method has been called a "theological historiography."[34] In one sense this is correct, since Pannenberg is trying to define a historical method that can be applied to actual events of God's revelation. On the other hand, however, Pannenberg is certainly not constructing a method that can be set over against or which competes with some so-called secular historiography. Because there is only one universal science of theology, there can be only one undifferentiated historiography—theological or otherwise. There is only one historical method by dint of the fact that ultimately every historical effort is theological—theological because history is God's self-revelation.

In summary, Pannenberg holds universal history to be ultimate reality, and all understanding of reality to be mediated by the historical process. Whatever methods may be used in determining the events of history must be in formal agreement with this view. Since God has revealed himself in the event of the fate and activity of Jesus, man is not free to put history outside of the most central categories of understanding. History *is* the most comprehensive horizon of a Christian theology.

## REVELATION

As noted in the first chapter, Pannenberg's concept of revelation takes for a starting point the understanding of revelation attributed to Hegel and Barth. Revelation is to be understood always as the self-revelation of God. As such it is not to be confused with either God himself or some static content. Just how it is to be considered is systematically expressed by Pannenberg in a series of "Dogmatic Theses on the Doctrine of Revelation." [35] These theses are the systematic conclusions of the Pannenberg circle's exegetical study of the Old and New Testaments' concept of revelation. They are crucial enough to merit listing before attempting to discuss their content.

Thesis 1: The self-revelation of God in the biblical witnesses is not of a direct type in the sense of a theophany, but is indirect and brought about by means of the historical acts of God.

Thesis 2: Revelation is not comprehended completely in the beginning, but at the end of the revealing history.

Thesis 3: In distinction from special manifestations of the deity, the historical revelation is open to anyone who has eyes to see. It has a universal character.

Thesis 4: The universal revelation of the deity of God is not yet realized in the history of Israel, but first in the fate of Jesus of Nazareth, insofar as the end of all events is anticipated in his fate.

Thesis 5: The Christ event does not reveal the deity of the God of Israel as an isolated event, but rather insofar as it is a part of the history of God with Israel.

Thesis 6: In the formulation of the non-Jewish conceptions of revelation in the gentile Christian church, the universality of the eschatological self-vindication of God in the fate of Jesus comes to actual expression.

Thesis 7: The Word relates itself to revelation as foretelling, forthtelling, and report.

Pannenberg regards the indirectness of revelation as the sure result of the investigation made into the concept of revelation in ancient Israel and primitive Christianity.[36] In both ancient Israel and primitive Christianity it was the historical activity of God that revealed God's deity and power. This historical activity could be either an event or a complex of events, but in each case it was still the events themselves that revealed God's deity and brought about belief. Even so eminent a theophany—a visible manifestation of God—as the person of Jesus did not reveal God as did historical events. God made his glory only indirectly visible in the fate rather than in the person of Jesus. Thus the self-revelation of God was and is an indirect presentation of himself by means of his historical acts. This understanding is of crucial importance and has far-reaching ramifications for Christian theology.

Not the least of these ramifications is the fact that if revelation is indirect, it follows that the comprehension of revelation must come at the end of the revealing history. Only after the completion of God's revealing history is his deity fully perceived. Thus revelation cannot be involved with single revelatory events. Revelation comes about through the series of occurrences which themselves continually revise the content of revelation until the completion of history when God's deity will be in full view. Each event is seen as only one step toward the always future full revelation of God. Pannenberg attributes this understanding to apocalyptic thought in Israel:

> It is not just the extent of events proving the deity of God that is increasing, but also the content of revelation that is continually revising itself. What had previously been the final vindication of God is now seen as only one step in the ever-increasing context of revelation.[37]

Since an understanding of the deity of God is based on the totality of all events, it is only at the end of history that God's revelation is known.

This view raises the question of how anything of God is known either in the past or the present. Pannenberg responds by pointing out that in the fate of Jesus the end of history is actually experienced in advance as an anticipation. In his fate, the end of history makes itself available to man. Since the resurrection, for example, is an actual historical event, it increases and revises the content of God's self-revelation made up until the resurrection. At the same time it bursts open all present categories of understanding such that it can only be understood in terms of the final resurrection of the

dead in the yet-to-come consummation. The fate of Jesus is
both past revelation and the anticipation of the end where
God fully reveals his deity through the totality of all events.
And in this sense the event of Jesus' fate provides the means
by which revelation is comprehended from the vantage point
of the end before the end.

But if the fate of Jesus is the anticipation of the totality
of all history, Christianity cannot be strictly limited to the
culture in which it began. "It is not by chance," says Pannenberg, "that the salvation now is for the Gentile also." [38] To
proclaim that the fate of Jesus is the anticipation of the end
of all history is to proclaim the "fundamental validity about
the way in which the theology of the ancient church developed
through the assimilation of the Greek spirit." [39] As the
Christian faith turned outward from its Jewish beginnings,
its further development within whatever environment is testimony that the fate of Jesus is an event that—while Jewish—
partakes of the universality of the end of history. Christianity's adaptation of Greek ideas is testimony to its universal
character.

The coming of Christianity to universality by its development in Greek culture illustrates the way God's self-revelation comes to be known. Since Christianity is a faith for all
men, God's revelation in the fate of Jesus is open for all men
to see. The special aspect of God's revelation is in the event
itself and not in some special attitude the recipient of revelation brings with him. Faith comes upon the open appropriation of the events of revelation, and thus salvation is open to
all who will see.

We come now to the special role Jesus plays in Pannenberg's concept of revelation. Since the fate of Jesus is the
sole anticipatory event of the end of history, Jesus stands as
the focal point of God's self-revelation. Pannenberg contends

that in the history of Israel Yahweh had not yet shown himself to be God for all men. Because of the limited scope of Israel's history and the incompleteness of all history God's revelation awaited a further development. This development came about in the rise of apocalypticism, a literary genre and mental set which saw history as always provisional and open to reinterpretation by the further acts of God. It was the genius of apocalypticism to insist upon the fact that even Yahweh's self-demonstration is always surpassed by new events until the end of all events. As a result the past is always being reopened for further understanding in light of the continuing events of God's revelation, and the present is always considered tentative in light of the future events that are swiftly coming. Only at the end of history is there anything resembling the final and complete revelation of God. This apocalyptic understanding forms the background into which Jesus came and by which he is understood.

Only with this background was it possible for the fate of Jesus to be understood as the already present end of all history. Not only is history always open to the future acts of God, but it is also the New Testament understanding that in the event of Jesus even the apocalyptic understanding is surpassed. Jesus is more than another event of indeterminate history. He is the actual end seen aforetime and experienced by his contemporaries as a "foretaste." Thus the event of Jesus both fulfills and breaks with a strictly Jewish understanding of God's revelation. By Jesus' identity with Jewish apocalypticism and at the same time his break with this tradition, "the universality of the eschatological self-vindication of God in the fate of Jesus comes to actual expression." [40]

As the universal revelation of God in the fate of Jesus penetrated the gentile world, gnostic thought—a type of thinking that was a peculiar admixture of philosophy and religion—played the role for the gentiles that apocalypticism had for the Jews. Since apocalyptic presuppositions were no longer understandable in the gentile environment, gnostic thought became the means by which the significance of the event of Jesus could be expressed. The assimilation of gnostic thinking by primitive Christian theology performed the function of making the God who raised Jesus from the dead intelligible as God to the gentile in the same fashion as the assimilation of apocalypticism performed the function of making God's activity in the history of Jesus intelligible to the Jew.

Pannenberg admits that some aspects of the biblical concept of revelation stand in opposition to the gnostic redeemer ideas.[41] Briefly, these are the points of opposition. (1) Gnosticism states that revelation occurs as direct communication from God; biblical thought maintains that revelation occurs indirectly through God's activity in history. (2) Gnosticism has revelation directed to the secret understanding or, in Christian gnosis, to faith; the biblical concept has God's revelation enacted openly before all eyes. And (3) the gnostic understanding of revelation involves the appearance of the divine in the human; the biblical understanding concentrates revelation in the fate of Jesus. Despite these evident contrasts, Pannenberg views the use of gnostic concepts by primitive Christian theology as entirely appropriate and necessary.

The appropriation of gnostic concepts in the development of Christian thought, however, is correct only as the "historical vindication of the deity of God in the fate of Jesus." [42] That is, while the appropriation illustrates that God's deity revealed in the fate of Jesus is a revelation of universal application, one cannot reverse the procedure so as to understand revelation in terms of gnostic concepts. The appropriation of gnostic concepts provides a cultural point of contact and a witness to the universality of the fate of Jesus of Nazareth, but it does not supply the content of revelation. In discussing the last thesis Pannenberg is concerned lest by designating revelation in history as "Word of God" this be understood to signify a "direct divine manifestation" after the gnostic definition of revelation. God involves himself "in the concrete execution of the history of revelation by means of his authorized word," but we must not confuse the function of "word" in revelation with the gnostic concept of a divine manifestation. For Pannenberg this raises the question then of how the authorized words of Yahweh and Jesus of Nazareth relate to the history which God activates. This relationship must be viewed from the context of the traditions and expectations within which the authorized words themselves appeared.

The authorized words relate to history first of all in terms of promise. When Israel experienced the self-vindication of Yahweh within certain events, it was usually in confirmation of words of promise or threat, as the case might be. This does not mean, of course, that the prophetic word spoken before the event was itself the self-vindication of God; it was only the vehicle of proclamation. There is a circularity involved here. As Pannenberg says, "The prophetic word precedes the act of history, and these acts are understandable as acts of Yahweh only because a statement coming in the name of Yahweh interprets them this way." [43] Yet the word is promise and not divine event.

The word of God is also understood to relate to history in terms of forthtelling. That is to say, the words of Yahweh in commandment and law already presuppose for their validity the deity and self-vindication of Yahweh in history. The word itself does not have the character of revelation but rather follows from the prior revelation of God.

Lastly, the word relates to history as kerygma in New Testament understanding. Pannenberg sees the kerygma or proclamation as essentially and exclusively the report of the revelation of God in the fate of Jesus. This is not to say that notification of men can be separated from the self-vindication of God in the fate of Jesus. But kerygma as a challenge or call to faith is not for that reason revelation itself. The kerygma is to be understood strictly in what it reports. And the same can be said of the church's proclamation. "The sermon as an event by itself is not revelation, but the report of the revealing history and an explication of the language of fact, which is implicit in this history." [44]

By these systematic expressions of the concept of revelation Pannenberg makes clear his commitment to the idea of universal history as the self-revelation of God. Revelation is history in all its many facets. The total mediation of meaning is through a history which is God made known. The dual problems of an indeterminate historical process and the Hegelian tendency of making absolute less than the total process are avoided strictly in terms of the fate of Jesus. Since his fate is a "before-the-end" anticipation of the end, the revelation of God in terms of total history can be known in the present; but the present always realizes the "yet-to-come" aspect of this future end of history. Thus man can live within a web of meaning that is incomplete and yet sufficient. He lives absolutely within the scheme of God's events without absolutizing the incomplete events of history. Man sees the self-revelation of God in the totality of the historical process —a totality which is given in the fate of Jesus.

## JESUS OF NAZARETH

As has been seen, the event of Jesus has key responsibilities in the framework of Pannenberg's thought. For this reason it is no surprise that Pannenberg's most extensive efforts at the presentation of a systematic theological concept have been in the area of the doctrine of Christ. His thought concerning the theological endeavor, history, and revelation dictates that the primary goal of the doctrine of Christ is to show the extent to which the history of Jesus constitutes the basis of faith in him.[45] The accomplishing of this goal is dependent upon two formal considerations—the methodology and the central content of the doctrine of Christ.

*Methodology*

Pannenberg delineates two possible approaches to the study of Christ—approaches which profoundly affect the content of the thought concerning him.[46] The first Pannenberg calls "christology from above"; the second, "christology from below." Christology from above is the more traditional of the two, beginning with Ignatius of Antioch and the second-century apologists. From these beginnings it became determinative for Western theology through the Alexandrian christology of Athanasius and Cyril. The primary modern exponent of this approach is Karl Barth.

For Barth christology from above emphasizes the divinity of Jesus and places the incarnation at the center of all theology. He is more interested in how the Christ is Jesus of Nazareth than in how Jesus of Nazareth is the Christ. As a consequence, Barth speaks about a "history" of the incarnation—the history of the Son of God going into what is foreign by becoming a man, by uniting himself with the man Jesus. It is upon this history rather than upon the history of the fate of Jesus that faith is grounded.[47]

Pannenberg, on the other hand, advocates a christology from below, which, "rising from the historical man Jesus to the recognition of his divinity, is concerned first of all with Jesus' message and fate and arrives only at the end at the

concept of the incarnation." [48] Pannenberg's preference for
this approach is based upon three weaknesses he sees in
christology from above.

First, christology from above assumes from the outset the
divinity of Jesus. The most important task of christology is
precisely that of presenting reasons for the confession of
Jesus' divinity rather than merely presupposing it. Second,
christology from above has great difficulty in properly
weighing the significance of the historical man, Jesus of
Nazareth. When viewed from above, the focus is already upon
the union between man and God, the very concept the events
of Jesus' life are supposed to present. And third, christology from above is tenable only if one can stand in the position
of God himself and follow the way of God's Son into the
world. Because of these weaknesses Pannenberg, with his
commitment to the "context of a historically determined
human situation," rules out this approach as a possibility. [49]

*Central Content*

Having supplied a formal method for the study of the
doctrine of Christ, Pannenberg turns his attention to the primary event in any study of Christ—the resurrection of Jesus.
It is here that the christology from below puts flesh on the
methodological bones. It was only because of the resurrection
of Jesus in the first place that the writers of the Gospels were
able to describe Jesus' cause as the cause of the Messiah.
Had it not been for the resurrection—considered in connection with Jesus' entire life—all the previous events of his life
would have been something else than they now are. Without
the resurrection christology would be an uncertain and in-
scrutable discipline.

The resurrection is the focus of christology; but it too, like
all other events of Jesus' history, must be approached from

below. That is to say, it must be seen as a historical event within the fabric of all other events. Only when its revelatory character is not something additional to the event can the resurrection provide the basis for faith. Only when the hard questions of historical facticity are met and not by-passed does the resurrection provide the basis of belief. This is the central issue with which christology from below must deal.

Pannenberg understands the historical problem of the resurrection of Jesus to revolve around two different strands of the Easter tradition in primitive Christianity—the appearances of the resurrected Lord and the idea of Jesus' empty tomb. It is around these two traditions that Pannenberg seeks to carry out the historical research necessary to validate the factuality of the resurrection of Jesus.

In carrying out the necessary historical research, Pannenberg makes implicit reference to two methodological principles which govern historical research. The recognition and acceptance of these principles determine whether a case for factuality can be made. Consequently, we need to be aware of them before approaching Pannenberg's research into the historical problem.

The first methodological necessity for the historian is a concept of history which does not rule out any possibility a priori. Some discussions of the possibility of Jesus' resurrection turn upon the argument that the resurrection of a dead person violates the laws of nature and is therefore impossible. Such an argument, however, cannot claim the authority of modern science, for science emphasizes that only a part of the laws of nature are ever known. Furthermore, although conformity to law represents one important aspect of individual events, no individual event is ever completely determined by the laws of nature. The laws of nature are themselves contingent, so that in principle no definitive judg-

ments about the possibility or impossibility of an event can
be made. The high probability of an event's occurrence or
nonoccurrence can never be transmuted into a statement of
factuality. Thus Pannenberg says, "The judgment about
whether an event, however unfamiliar, has happened or not
is in the final analysis a matter for the historian and cannot
be prejudged by the knowledge of natural science." [50]

The second methodological principle affirms that if an
event can be shown to be the most adequate historical explanation of the circumstances surrounding the event in question, that event must be considered historically very probable.
And this historical probability "always means in historical
inquiry that it (the event) is to be presupposed until contrary evidence appears." [51] The particular significance of
this principle is in the recognition that historical knowledge
can never consist of more than a statement that an event has a
high degree of probability. Although a probable event, even
a highly probable one, is always in principle open to further
evidence, the procedure of historical research demands that
the assertion of a probable event's reality be sustained until
contrary evidence appears. The historian does not have to
have nor can he supply indubitable proof of an event. He
simply must demonstrate that the reality of an event is the
most probable explanation of the circumstances.

With these two principles clearly in mind Pannenberg
analyzes the evidence for the reality of the resurrection, first
of all, with regard to the appearance tradition. This is a
tradition amply attested in both Gospel and Pauline writing.
However, 1 Corinthians 15:1–11 is of especial significance,
since the account of the appearances of the resurrected Lord
given in this passage dates from a much earlier time than the
accounts given in the Gospels. It also avoids the heavily
colored approach taken by the Gospel writers in underlining

the corporeality of the resurrected Lord in his appearances. That the reported appearances are not mere fabrications "freely invented in the course of later legendary development" is attested, in Pannenberg's understanding, by the person of Paul and by the age of the formula in which the appearances are reported.[52] In the account in 1 Corinthians 15, Paul is undoubtedly speaking from personal experience in reciting the appearance of the resurrected Lord to him. Furthermore, the account of the appearances to the others and particularly to James must have become known to Paul —perhaps by personal interview in Jerusalem after his conversion—not later than six to eight years after the events themselves. Thus in reciting the occurrences of the appearances, Paul is not speaking from secondary evidence, that is, from later reports of some supposed experiences. He is speaking from his personal experience of an appearance and from evidence very close to the other appearances themselves.

That the appearances have good historical foundation is further attested by the fact that Paul uses a formulation of the kerygma coined much earlier than the writing of 1 Corinthians in about A.D. 56. This is a formulation coined independently of Paul. Thus Paul does not create a statement of the appearances for the sake of his argument at the moment. Rather he appeals to an already formulated record of the appearances. Since this formulation was received by Paul, it must stand even closer to the events of the appearances than the six to eight years mentioned previously. The net result of this investigation is the conclusion that the appearances of the resurrected Lord to the disciples and others is the most likely explanation of the appearance tradition. Since the tradition arose at such an early date and independently of Paul's argument, the most probable explanation of the circumstances is that the appearances actually occurred.

This is only half of the necessary historical investigation, however, for even if the appearances of the resurrected Lord are historically verified, further investigation is necessary before these appearances can be accepted as historical evidence of the resurrection. Pannenberg undertakes this difficult task by delving into the content and the character of the Easter appearances.

With regard to the content of the appearances it is evident from 1 Corinthians 15 that Paul regarded the appearance to him as being the same kind of appearance as those to the other apostles. And from an analysis of Paul's own statements in Galatians 1:12 and 16 at least one fact is certain. It is Jesus of Nazareth who appears in the experiences. This is the assured content of the appearances.

This assurance makes very crucial the matter of the character of the appearances. If they can be dismissed as the highly subjective imagination of an unstable mind, then they offer no historical verification of the resurrection. It is with this argument in mind that Pannenberg agrees that the appearances can only be best described as vision experiences. The use of the term *vision*, however, need not mean that the experiences have no extrasubjective reality. The many attempts at explaining the appearances of Jesus of Nazareth to the disciples according to the "subjective vision hypothesis" have repeatedly failed. Such views consistently fail to give account of the Easter faith of the disciples and experience great difficulty in accounting for the number and the temporal distribution of the appearances.

In the final analysis, according to Pannenberg, the most satisfying explanation of all these circumstances is to speak "not only of the visions of Jesus' disciples but also of appearances of the resurrected Jesus." [53] Such speech will of course be metaphorical, but this need not hinder us "from understanding the course of events with the help of what is designated by such language when other possibilities for explanation remain unsatisfactory." [54]

From these considerations Pannenberg concludes that the resurrection of Jesus is the most likely explanation of the various circumstances. In that sense the resurrection is to be "designated as a historical event. . . . If the emergence of primitive Christianity . . . traced back by Paul to appearances of the resurrected Jesus, can be understood . . . only if one examines it in the light of the eschatological hope for a resurrection from the dead, then that which is so designated is a historical event, even if we do not know anything more particular about it." [55]

The second strand of Easter tradition which Pannenberg investigates is that of Jesus' empty tomb. The earliest stratum of the Gospel materials indicates that this tradition was early and prominent in the primitive Christian community of Jerusalem. Not only is this tradition early, but it appears to have existed for a period in isolation from the appearance tradition, as is indicated by the fact that the earliest Gospel, Mark, presents only the empty tomb tradition when reporting the resurrection. It is only in later Gospels and in the spurious ending to Mark that there is an attempt to combine the two traditions.

That the empty tomb tradition pointed to a fact is substantiated by the fact that the Jewish polemic—part of which is evident within the New Testament itself—did not deny the empty tomb. The polemic argued that the disciples had stolen the body but not that the tomb had been lost or was still filled. Furthermore, the situation in Jerusalem demanded that there be reliable evidence that the tomb was actually empty. The early church's proclamation of the resurrection could not have survived a single day had not the emptiness of the tomb been an established fact. Thus that the proclamation of the empty tomb continued to survive is further evidence that the tomb actually was empty.

These considerations do not, of course, prove the resurrection by a formal type of proof. But if the empty tomb tradition arose independently of the appearance tradition, as Pannenberg believes, "then by their mutually complementing each other they let the assertion of the reality of Jesus' resurrection . . . appear as historically very probable." [56] This is the type of evidence with which all historical research must deal. If the historian does not rule out the possibility of resurrection a priori, the reality of the resurrection is the most probable explanation of the development and continuation of these two traditions. Pannenberg concludes upon this basis that "the event of the resurrection of Jesus is an historical event, an event that really happened at that time." [57] Until evidence to the contrary is presented, the historian will maintain this position as the most probable explanation.

For theological purposes, however, it is not sufficient simply to indicate the evidence for the historical reality of the resurrection. Something also needs to be said concerning its significance. In so doing Pannenberg reminds us that the expression "resurrection from the dead" is metaphorical in nature. An analysis of the scriptural uses of this concept convinces Pannenberg that what is involved here is a reality quite apart from the reality expressed by the miracles of revivification. This being the case, the positive aspect of analogy in historical research dictates the "resurrection" be regarded as a symbolic, metaphorical name for a reality unique to human experience. Yet, in order to maintain knowledge of this reality it is placed in juxtaposition to the New Testament concept of the general resurrection of the dead in the last times. The closeness of this connection is seen

in 1 Corinthians 15:16, where Paul makes "the expectation of
the general resurrection of the dead the presupposition of the
acknowledgment of Jesus' resurrection." [58]

At this point in his discussion of the resurrection, Pannenberg puts the actuality of the resurrection together with its
meaning. Since the resurrection of Jesus was and is a unique
event, it can only be understood in its original context of the
apocalyptic final resurrection of the dead. Thus the resurrection is at one and the same time tied to the past and the
future. The connection to its original context allows the resurrection to signify the necessity of a continued historical
consciousness. The connection to its future allows it to signify
the anticipation of the end of history. Precisely both these
aspects are necessary if the resurrection is the basis of faith.

The future aspect of the resurrection has special significance for Pannenberg. It is the future connection of the resurrection that makes it revelation for us. For "only in
connection with the end of the world that still remains to
come can what has happened in Jesus through his resurrection from the dead possess and retain the character of revelation for us." [59] Since the revelation of God comes only at the
end of history, it is absolutely necessary—if there is to be
revelation at all—for the end of history to be already available to the present.

Since for Pannenberg man is man by virtue of the fact
that he is "open to the world," man cannot ignore the resurrection, the event which alone opens to him the historical
process and thereby saves him. [60] The resurrection antici-
pates the end and thereby calls man to commit himself to
God upon the basis of the revelation of God in the totality of
history. Pannenberg concludes:

Therefore, now man's attitude towards Jesus as a man is decisive for his future destiny, this was the claim made by Jesus before the events in Jerusalem. Thus, man has a hope beyond death through community with Jesus. In his destiny the final destiny of all men became an event, and through this Jesus proclaimed that the destiny of all people will be decided by the attitude they have toward him.[61]

Theologically, the resurrection of Jesus is the final revelation of God by which can be affirmed the divinity of Jesus. This divinity makes clear the inner meaning of the resurrection; it does not, however, add anything essential to the event itself. The resurrection is a historical reality. It is the appearance of the end of history by means of which the whole process of history has been opened as the revelation of God himself. It is upon this revelation that man bases his life in faith toward the God of the future.

## A CONCLUDING WORD

In concluding this section on the central motifs of Pannenberg's thought, we must remember that the motifs presented certainly do not exhaust Pannenberg's thought. All that can be claimed for the concepts dealt with is that they are representative of and central to Pannenberg's thought at the present. Difficult as they are, they serve the purpose of delineating some basic ideas of Pannenberg's theology.

# III. Pannenberg
# in Dialogue

In 1964 an analysis of the theological scene announced Pannenberg as one of three theologians who already marked the new directions of continental theology since 1960. According to this analysis, Pannenberg, Gerhard Ebeling, and Heinrich Ott were the three theologians providing the really new directions in theology.[1] Certainly, as Pannenberg has continued to write, it has become evident that he is at least providing an alternative to the current theological tendencies. Pannenberg's new direction in the ongoing task of theological reflection will, at the least, provide a basis for theological debate.

Before making too much of this idea of a "new direction" provided by Pannenberg, a word of caution is necessary. This idea should not be misread in such fashion as to obscure Pannenberg's historical continuity with and dependence upon the earlier forms of continental theology. Neither is Pannenberg isolated from current theological movements. He is thoroughly involved in the overall theological task, as has already been attested in our first chapter. Our purpose at this point is to examine exactly how Pannenberg engages the major assumptions of contemporary theological thought.

## HERMENEUTICAL THEOLOGY

The first theological current to which we turn our attention is one containing several different schools of thought. For our purposes here, however, the term *hermeneutical* serves the purpose of pinpointing a common element among these schools and a basic assumption with which Pannenberg takes exception. Hermeneutical theology is an attempt—following a tradition at least as old as Luther—to speak theologically in the present, while remaining faithful to ancient but authoritative texts. Basic to this attempt are some very definite assumptions.

Hermeneutical theology first assumes that the New Testament—often the Old Testament and noncanonical writings are included as well—is normative for the Christian faith. What the New Testament writers had to say is important and valid for Christian theology. Bultmann articulates this position when on the last page of his *Theology of the New Testament* he affirms that the presupposition of his interpretation of the New Testament writings is "that they have something to say to the present." [2] Whatever variations in interpretation of the text may occur from theologian to theologian, agreement upon this point is certain—*these texts* are normative for the Christian faith.[3]

The second assumption of hermeneutical theology is that the theological task of unfolding faith's understanding of God must be carried out anew in every age. This assumption was evident as long ago as Schleiermacher's *Speeches on Religion to Its Cultured Despisers*, a work first published in

1799.[4] It continues to be a determining concern for herme-neutical theology.

The third assumption is actually a part of the other two; and yet, it is distinguishable. If the Scriptures are somehow significant for the Christian faith and if the theological task is that of actualizing their meaning in the present, then how is this task to be accomplished in light of a well-defined and well-publicized historical gap? The rise of a historical con-sciousness in the West and the development of certain theo-logical ideas have firmly convinced theology of the deep and abiding difference between biblical times and our own. The times are different, and they stand in tension with each other in the theologian's task of interpreting the texts.

Hermeneutical theology sees theology's task as that of somehow bridging the gap between the past and the present. That which is theologically important in the past must be brought into the present situation of man. An example of this concern is that type of theological activity which suggests that theology is basically the task of giving expression to what the text "meant" and what it "means," respectively.[5] In this understanding theology is two-pronged, having to do with past and present meaning. It is the bridging of the times.

For our purposes here three types of hermeneutical theol-ogy will set in relief Pannenberg's position. Pannenberg has learned much from these types of theological reflection, both in their presentation of the theological problem and in their characteristic solutions to the problem. By and large, however, he remains unconvinced. Too much is surrendered by the various ways the problem is solved.

*Karl Barth's Solution*

In his *Epistle to the Romans* and in the monumental *Church Dogmatics*, Karl Barth approaches the differences be-

tween the biblical past and our present by suggesting that
these differences have already been overcome in the fact of
the self-revelation of God.[6] The datum of revelation—God
himself—is such that it forever comes to man unconditioned
by the times. Any historical difference between the living
Word, the written Word, and the preached Word is superseded by the *fact* of the "Word." The Word, then, bridges the
historical differences between the times, because it is the
self-revelation of God who is not subject to man's time at all.

This does not mean that the difference between the biblical
past and the present of man has no significance for Barth.
Although the gap between the times is already bridged by
the fact of revelation, it remains visible as a testimony of the
human situation. The remoteness of the scriptural time is
symptomatic of man's remoteness from God; the nearness of
the revelation of God is symptomatic of the nearness of God's
grace. In this way the tension between our present and the
time of Scripture is resolved, or better still, transformed into
an expression of the relationship that exists between God and
man. But this transformation results in a depreciation of the
times themselves. The past and the present and the difference
between them are only metaphors pointing to a more crucial
time of God's revelation. Since God's self-revelation does
not occur within man's history, neither the time of past events
nor the time of the present enters in a constitutive way into
God's self-revelation.

The separation of man's time and God's time is adroitly
accomplished by Barth through the utilization of two German words for history—*Geschichte* and *Historie*. Our time
in its radical brokenness is *Historie*. God's time is *Geschichte*.
The tension between past and present evident in *Historie* is
overcome and redeemed by *Geschichte*.[7] This is again another
way of saying that the distance between past and present is

superseded in that the Christian is caught up into a special redemptive history wherein he is confronted by God. The tension between the past and the present is that of a perverted history already overcome by the history of God's self-revelation.

This scheme results in dual histories, which in turn produce a revelation apart from the history of man, a history of revelation separate from secular history, and a resolution of the tension between then and now by means of a disengagement of the time of revelation from man's history. Thus the tension between the past and the present becomes only a paradigm of "fallen" time, and the theologian lives in a world separated from the world of man's history. In the final analysis man's history is not and cannot be God's history.

The results of this theological position Pannenberg finds uncongenial in at least two respects. First, when Barth separates revelation from the biblical past understood as man's history and locates it in a special history of God, he effectively by-passes the need for historical critical study of the Bible. What actually happened in the biblical past is only accidentally related to the revelation of God in Jesus Christ, and a critical approach to the documents of this biblical past is rendered less than mandatory. If the self-revelation of God is not located within the history of man, a critical historical study is not absolutely necessary. Or, to say it another way, if the self-revelation of God is not the history of man, critical historical study is only of casual interest to the theologian. It is precisely this casual interest that Pannenberg cannot accept as normative for the theological endeavor.[8]

A second result of Barth's theological formulations with which Pannenberg takes strong exception is the conscious attempt to separate theology's content from the normal concourse of human activity. For Barth, the theologian is exclusively interested in a special history of revelation by means of which the Christian is related to God. In this special realm the reason of man is little more than an expression of man's basic sinfulness. This understanding violates Pannenberg's rationality. The positing of a special separate history beyond man's understanding decimates the basic premises of understanding—premises Pannenberg sees as given in revelation itself. Theology's content occurs in and as the history of man, and in doing so it is open to man's understanding. Theology's subject matter dictates that the theologian cannot escape into a realm where he does not have to submit himself and his thought processes to the rigors of rationality.[9]

Thus Pannenberg's conscious commitment to reason does not allow the luxury of fragmenting reality into two histories. The ground for this commitment to reason Pannenberg sees adequately attested in biblical monotheism and incarnation. Since God is one and has revealed himself through the history of Jesus of Nazareth, theology must insist upon a unified reality and forbid any attempt at ghettoizing theology by shutting it off from the common arena of thought. Theology must deal with this one world of man's history in a radically historical way.

## Rudolf Bultmann's Solution

Another hermeneutical theologian with whom Pannenberg often finds himself in serious discussion is Rudolf Bultmann. Bultmann's solution to the problem of bridging the distance between the biblical past and man's present places him squarely within the traditions of historical critical study of the Scriptures. He does so with the purpose of delineating two different approaches to the New Testament. Either the New Testament writings can be "interrogated as the 'sources' which the historian interprets in order to reconstruct a picture of primitive Christianity as a phenomenon of the historical past," or else they can be interrogated as to how the historian's picture "stands in the service of the interpretation of the New Testament writings." [10] Because he presupposes that the New Testament writings have something to say to the present, Bultmann chooses the latter approach. Up to this point Pannenberg is in full agreement.

Bultmann continues his analysis of the New Testament to assert that what the New Testament has to say to the present is quite apart from the subject matter of the New Testament writings, that is, apart from the events of history which the writings ostensibly report. The New Testament writings "can claim to have meaning for the present not as theoretical teachings, timeless general truths, but only as the expression of an understanding of human existence which for the man of today also is a possibility for his understanding of himself— a possibility which is opened to him by the New Testament itself, in that it not only shows him that such self-understanding is a reply to the kerygma as the word of God addressing him, but also imparts to him the kerygma itself." [11]

Thus Bultmann resolves the tension between the then and now by having the text express "an understanding of human existence" which is also the potential for present man's coming to self-understanding. The Scripture text presents not history but an understanding of human existence which is valid for the present. To approach the text as a witness to the events of the historical past is for Bultmann a hopelessly unfruitful task. Rather the task of theology is to make clear the reference of present man's believing self-understanding to the proclamation of Christ. The "something" the New Testament has to say to the present is to be found strictly within the context of this believing self-understanding.

When Bultmann thus locates revelation outside the historical arena of actual events and in the past and present self-
understanding of man, Pannenberg's most basic assumption
is violated. Reality for Pannenberg is historical and the revelation of God comes in terms of and as witness to that reality.
To dehistoricize revelation by locating it in a nonhistorical
self-understanding which transcends the vicissitudes of the
historical process is as unacceptable as is Barth's call for a
theology which builds upon a history immunized against
man's understanding. The historical distance between the biblical past and man's present cannot be adequately bridged
by allowing present man's concept of self-understanding to
dictate a view of the texts of the New Testament which
effectively negates their claim to and tie with the history of
Jesus of Nazareth.

## Oscar Cullmann's Solution

The third solution to the problem of bridging the distance
between the then and now is that of Oscar Cullmann and
points up another tendency in hermeneutical theology with
which Pannenberg differs. Although Pannenberg agrees with
Cullmann as to the centrality of the concepts of time and
history in the New Testament thought world, he feels that
Cullmann fails theologically on two counts.[12]

First, Cullmann is philosophically naïve, when in describ-
ing the thought processes of the New Testament writers he
assumes these thought processes either can or should be the
categories of modern thought. Even if Cullmann can adequately demonstrate through exegesis that the primary concept of the biblical writers is a rectilinear view of time, this
in no way demonstrates that modern man can or should view
time as a rectilinear process. The second failure arises out of
the first. Not only must the theologian analyze and describe

biblical thought, but he must also give some indication of how this thought can be meaningful and decisive for the present. Lacking any penetrating philosophical analysis of reality that might serve as a point of contact with the present, Cullmann fails precisely at this point.

Pannenberg consciously sets about the tasks that Cullmann unconsciously leaves undone. Accepting the basic centrality of time and history as New Testament concepts, Pannenberg applies these concepts to the pressing question of today. He makes his exegetical claims within and toward a comprehensive philosophical structure in order to avoid the failure of being merely descriptive. This approach prevents him from becoming simply an antiquarian, that is, one interested in history—even biblical history—purely for the sake of history. Thus for Pannenberg theology must be the ground for all understanding and not primarily the cataloging of exegetical results.

Pannenberg also addresses himself to the questions of interpretation and meaning frequently left unanswered by Cullmann. Since it is not enough to assume that the biblical concepts are meaningful without considerable effort given to translating them into the present, Pannenberg supplies the very principles of interpretation which are necessary to the proper doing of the theological task. Thus Pannenberg can affirm equally with Cullmann the centrality of certain concepts, such as a certain view of time, and at the same time provide the principles of interpretation which can meaningfully actualize those concepts for modern man.[13]

There are some additional disagreements between Cullmann and Pannenberg which stem from differences in exegesis. For example, Cullmann sees Jesus as the midpoint of history, the point at which God's purpose is already essentially accomplished. Subsequent history is the time for the outworking of the victory already won in Christ. Pannenberg on the other hand sees in the fate of Jesus the anticipation of the future end of history in its completion. History after Jesus is the expression of the dynamic of the future already made available in Jesus. Cullmann sees Jesus as the temporal midpoint; Pannenberg sees Jesus as the temporal end. These differences are not, however, as decisive as the differences in approach to the theological task already discussed.

*Summary*

In Pannenberg's opposition to these various emphases in hermeneutical theology we see his characteristic concepts setting him apart from a mainstream of theological activity. Although he is in agreement with some of the ideas prominent in hermeneutical theology, Pannenberg finds that each of the approaches examined is unacceptable. Pannenberg wants a unity to reality absent in Barth, a historicity of reality absent in Bultmann, and a philosophical awareness absent in Cullmann.

For Pannenberg, theology cannot be a discipline carried on in a realm apart from the normal sphere of human activity—a realm in which faith is active apart from the rational capacities of man. This is the Barthian error. Neither can theology be primarily translated into categories of existential awareness. To do so is to give determinative priority to the categories of the present and to fail to give proper weight to the biblical category of history. This is the Bultmannian error. And last, theology cannot be content merely to recount the biblical categories without the epistemological awarenesses necessary since Kant and the Enlightenment. It is this inadequacy that is Cullmann's error.

To each of these characteristic emphases Pannenberg gives

a negative response in terms of his own theological convictions. For him theology is a universal science based upon the facticity of the events of scriptural record. It is out of this actual history of Jesus that theological statements must come.

## POLITICAL THEOLOGY

Another aspect of the theological spectrum which engages Pannenberg's thought is political theology. The designation is used here to refer to several theological emphases which have variously been labeled by such titles as theology of hope, theology of the future, secular theology, theology of revolution, and so forth. To group these different emphases together under the heading "political theology" is not to say there are no legitimate differences between them. Rather it is to say that there is a common element among them—an element sufficiently discernable as to mark it as a focus in contemporary theology.

The common element that marks this focus in contemporary theology is a new style of theological endeavor—a style which sets its proponents apart from the more familiar hermeneutical theology of the first half of this century. While it would be possible to characterize this theological style by one of several prominent ideas, such as "hope" or "secularity," to do so is to misread the intent of the theologians involved. "Hope" or "secularity" or other such ideas are but different ways into a more comprehensive thought structure in which, to differing degrees, all participate.

This more comprehensive thought structure is political theology, taken in the traditional, Aristotelian sense of the term *political*. This approach sees the traditional theological categories as most understandable and meaningful when taken within the context of man's responsibility toward life, culture, and society and within the inner dynamics of this responsibility.[14] For Aristotle, "politics" referred to "the science of the polis," the science of securing the highest good for the city-state. Thus political theology is used to refer to man's "activity, and reflection on activity, which aims at and analyzes what it takes to make and keep human life human in the world." [15]

## Cultural Point of Contact

The principals of political theology have taken seriously the need to relate their understandings to a cultural point of contact. For several of them this point of contact has been the philosophy of hope sketched by the octogenarian Marxist, Ernst Bloch. Bloch published his monumental and difficult *Das Prinzip Hoffnung* in 1959, after moving from East Germany. Although Bloch is an atheist, at least on his own terms, his analysis of man has provided the point of contact with the modern world that political theology must have in order to survive as a live option according to its own criteria.

For Bloch, man is constituted by the hope which he holds for the future of humanity and the world. Man's primary tense is the future, that which is not yet. Man is man only as his life remains open-ended toward the future. This open-endedness is evidenced by hope. The new, the possibility of becoming, the future, and hope—all these serve as basic categories in Bloch's ontology of "not-yet-being."

Bloch, when challenged to capsulize his philosophy in one sentence, dared to attempt it with the statement, "S is not yet P." [16] This indicates, among other things, that what is, is becoming something else. This idea renders the revered law of identity passé and at the same time opens a whole new world in which creativity and novelty are not mere functions of man's traditions, past or present. The future is not bound to be only an expression of past and present tendencies. It is "not-yet-being" toward which man relates by means of hope. From this philosophical underpinning, political theology is currently busy drawing out implications for a theology that is eschatological in its emphasis on hope, the future, open-endedness, and novelty. These concepts, of course, are not new in themselves to theology. Rather it is their application that provides the new focus of political theology.

Often hermeneutical theology has been primarily interested in applying the meaning of Scripture to the individual believer's subjectivity; political theology is interested in applying meaning to the structures of political life. Hermeneutical theology has often been most interested in the manner of man's existence in the world. Political theology is most interested in the responsibility inherent in man's hopes for the world. This responsibility has more affinity for the social dimensions of freedom, power, revolution, and so on, than it does for individual salvation, faith, happiness, or authentic existence. Thus the theologians building upon Bloch's philosophy are apt to view the true nature of Christianity as consisting more in action in the social arena than in static individual adjustment. For this reason many of the traditional categories of Christian thought are reinterpreted in terms of the impact of man's hope upon the present becomingness of the world.

## *Jürgen Moltmann's Theology of Hope*

Two theologians will serve to illustrate how political theology comes to expression in contemporary theological thought. The more overtly theological of the two is Jürgen Moltmann, a contemporary German theologian. His primary work to date is a book entitled *Theology of Hope*. This title's close parallel to the title of Bloch's principal work hints at the usage Moltmann makes of Bloch's thought as a cultural point of contact.[17]

Moltmann affirms the impossibility of taking over the secular form of hope expounded by Bloch, but he does takes "hope" as the key and motive proper for the theological task.[18] Although Bloch credits the Bible with providing man's "eschatological consciousness," Moltmann affirms Bloch's "hope without faith" to be in the final analysis "a humanism without God." In contrast to this humanism, Moltmann intends to rediscover the "logos of hope" inherent in Christian eschatology. For Moltmann, Christian theology is primarily a hope that is always looking and moving forward, and in so doing, it transforms and revolutionizes the present. "The eschatological," says Moltmann, "is not one element *of* Christianity, but it is the medium of Christian faith as such, the key in which everything in it is set, the glow that suffuses everything here in the dawn of an expected new day." [19]

According to Moltmann the one real problem of Christian theology is the problem of the future. An examination of the Old and New Testaments reveals that God has made himself known as a God whose essential nature is future. God is no "intra-worldly or extra-worldly God"; but rather he is the God who is always only before us, a God who encounters us in his promises for the future.

This raises the very real problem of how the theologian in the present is to speak of the God of the future in concepts and words of the present. Since the future is not merely an extension or continuation of the present, present concepts and words are always inappropriate to the future. Moltmann concludes that one in reality never speaks of the future as such. The future can only be announced.

Thus eschatology begins from a definite reality in history

and announces the future of that reality. The announced future itself has power over the future in as much as the announcement calls man to the realization of that which is announced. In this sense Christian eschatology speaks only of Jesus Christ and his future. The resurrection is testimony that the crucified one has a future. It points believers to his future, a future already in the world in terms of promise.

In Jesus Christ the hidden future "announces itself and exerts its influence on the present through the hope it awakens." Theological statements can never be only descriptions of the existing reality but must rather be announcements of the reality which is coming. In Moltmann's words, theology does not "seek to bear the train of reality, but to carry the torch before it." [20] And for this reason the future can never be drawn into harmony with the present, standing as it does as the expression of the contradiction seen in the cross and the resurrection.

Since the future contradicts the present, the nature of hope is to draw the believer out of a "god-forsaken, transient reality" into the future of Jesus Christ which has been announced by the resurrection. "Hence eschatology," writes Moltmann, "must formulate its statements of hope in contradiction to our present experience of suffering, evil and death." [21]

For Moltmann, then, hope is the inseparable companion of faith. In the resurrection the boundary of all human hope —death—is broken open by the promise of the future of Jesus Christ. In terms of this promise, faith expands into hope, a hope which "sets this faith open to the comprehensive future of Christ." Thus faith in Christ is a recognition of the dawning of his future, a recognition which in turn opens to the believer new horizons.

The man who thus hopes is never able to reconcile himself

to the constraints of the present time and the present world. For him the resurrection is God's contradiction of this life of suffering and death. It is the opening of a future—Jesus Christ's future—which makes it impossible to endorse present reality. "Peace with God means conflict with the world, for the goal of the promised future stabs inexorably into the flesh of every unfulfilled present." [22] Thus the primary goal of the believer becomes the transformation of the present reality in expectation of the divine transformation in the future.

This brief sketch of Moltmann's thought is incomplete but will be adequate for the task of relating it to Pannenberg's theological formulations. Often Moltmann and Pannenberg are quoted together as examples of the same theological type.[23] And indeed there are several aspects of their thought which are terminologically the same. With Moltmann, Pannenberg speaks of the "God of hope," and emphasizes the key role the future plays in a Christian theology.[24] There is, however, a basic difference in outlook that obviates these linguistic similarities. This difference is recognized by Moltmann himself in his hearty criticisms of Pannenberg.

First, Moltmann contends that Pannenberg's theology of universal history is an attempt to replace the Greek cosmic proof for God with an eschatological or historical one. Second, Moltmann contends that Pannenberg's concept of revelation as history misses the decisive question of Cartesian and Kantian thought, namely, how the distinction between reality and the perception of reality is to be overcome. And third, Moltmann feels that to view the resurrection of Jesus as the anticipation of the end of universal history is to produce a completed history of Jesus which contradicts the biblical understanding of the cross. For Moltmann the cross stands as a reminder of the continuing contradiction of the present by the power of the future.[25]

Moltmann concludes his extensive criticism of Pannenberg with the affirmation that "the theologian is not concerned merely to supply a different *interpretation* of the world, of history and of human nature, but to *transform* them in expectation of a divine transformation." [26] This statement precisely points out the difference between Pannenberg and Moltmann and indicates why Moltmann's foregoing criticisms of Pannenberg tend to confuse rather than clarify the issue between them.

The basic difference between Pannenberg and Moltmann lies in their views of reality and the theologian's task in relation to it. For Pannenberg it is the theologian's task to interpret reality as made known in the fate of Jesus. He sees in the biblical witness to the fate of Jesus the key to the proper ontology, that is, to the proper understanding of the God-created reality. For Moltmann, on the other hand, the only reality available is the reality of "not-yet-being." Present reality is always contradicted by the future which is not yet. The theologian's task is that of transforming the present in light of the contradiction by the future which is promised but not yet come. There is no reality of the future, only the reality of "not-yet-being."

Moltmann, following Bloch, makes "not-yet-being" the basic reality of this world, whereas Pannenberg does not. The "not-yet" in Pannenberg's thought is a function and characteristic of historical reality, but it is not that reality itself. The "not-yet" is not completely future, having already arrived in the appearance of Jesus. Consequently, the Christian community stands to affirm and interpret the reality which has already arrived in Jesus' fate.

Thus, underlying the difference between Pannenberg and Moltmann is a difference in their views of reality. Pannenberg makes the historical process the real; Moltmann makes the tendency of the present toward that which is yet to come the real. By including the future in this historical process which is the full revelation of God, Pannenberg rescues the future from unreality, from being an abstraction based upon the analysis of what appears to be. The failure to do this is regarded by Pannenberg as an error of understanding—an error Moltmann does not sufficiently guard against.

This error is examined in Pannenberg's article "Appearance as the Arrival of the Future." [27] In this article Pannenberg discusses the problem presented by the word *appearance*, and concludes that since Parmenides—an ancient Greek philosopher who emphasized the absoluteness of being— the tendency of man has been to universalize, and thereby to absolutize, his abstractions. Faced with the infinite multiplicity of events, man feels threatened. In consequence, he asserts himself against this threat by constructing a constant and secure element in the present. He makes this element supreme. But Pannenberg asks, "Is not man seeking an absolute confirmation of himself in the apotheosis of what always is?" [28]

Moltmann's constant element is more sophisticated than many. Where some have made "being" the repeated and absolute element underlying the multitude of events, Moltmann makes "not-yet-being" or "becoming" the absolute. This only is constant amidst the flux. But, for Pannenberg, even "becoming," when made universal, can only be an absolute confirmation of man himself. It is an absolutizing of what always is. And this approach is improper, according to Pannenberg.

Only if the phenomenon of "becoming" itself is the arrival of God's future, that is, is historical in structure, can one avoid the worship of what is. Only if contingency itself stems from a completed future is one able to avoid absolutizing an element of the present. Pannenberg feels he avoids these pitfalls by affirming that the contingency of any event is the result of the fact that the future *"wills* to become present." The present does not affirm a tendency toward the future; the future grants an openness toward the future to every present. In this way the contingency of every present event does not abrogate itself in being affirmed. The future guarantees that the present can remain contingent.

## Harvey Cox's Celebration of Secularity

A more popular and less technical form of political theology is found in the writings of Harvey Cox. Since the phenomenal popularity of *The Secular City* in 1965, Cox has been a leader of that type of political theology marked by the celebration of secularity.[29]

Cox announces the coming of secularization as the "legitimate consequence of the impact of biblical faith on history."[30] The dimensions of secularization, for example, are revealed in the disenchantment of nature arising from the creation, the desacralization of politics arising from the Exodus, and the deconsecration of values arising from the Sinai Covenant.[31] Each of these dimensions began in biblical faith and culminates in the urbanization of this age. The outcome is that man is responsible for the world of nature and has been given mastery over and responsibility in the sphere of world affairs.

To speak theologically within this world is to speak of politics rather than metaphysics. Theological speech consists of "reflection-in-action by which the church finds out what this politician-God is up to and moves in to work along with him."[32] God is not to be conceived of as a transcendent being.

Rather Cox is concerned to present a picture of God—Cox
accepts this concern as one form of the "death of God" idea
—which is not a picture at all in the sense of the identification
of a transcendent God with the controlling symbols of our
culture. The need is for a contemporary form of thinking
about God which begins "with the recognition that man now
sees himself as the one who can and must carry through many
of the responsibilities which men of earlier millennia have
assigned to their gods." [33]

Cox regards Ernst Bloch as the most seminal mind capable of lighting the way in a time when pluralism and radical
historicism have become the constant companions of theology.
Bloch's analysis of reality is the most viable philosophical partner for theology in our time. His emphasis on the future means that the Christian God must be a God who "will
be" rather than a God who "is." Thus for Cox theology must
turn its attention "to that future which God makes possible
but for which man is inescapably responsible." [34]

Following Bloch, Cox advocates a political approach to
theology which is in harmony with the following ideas. (1)
Theology is primarily a function of life in this world and not
an exercise in transcendentalism. (2) As a function of life in
this world, theology emphasizes the radical pluralization and
de-ultimatization of the institutions of this life. (3) This
emphasis speaks emphatically of man's responsibility to act
in order to shape, form, and mold his world. Thus the Christian's task is to further the secularization process precisely
where it has not yet come to completion.

Pannenberg's relationship to the thought of Cox is not un-
ambiguous. Several of Pannenberg's emphases closely parallel
the results of Cox's thought concerning the theological task.
Pannenberg is appreciative of Cox's emphasis upon the responsibility of man in this world and the need of the present

for the transforming power of the future. And yet there is a profound difference between the two men.

The crux of this difference is the concept of the kingdom of God.[35] For Pannenberg the kingdom is "the *coming reality*"; for Cox the kingdom may be said to be the *coming*. To Pannenberg, the biblical literature is so understood as to indicate a future coming kingdom which is never attained in any present moment. The kingdom stands in the future, demanding obedience and action already in the present because of the dynamic of historical reality enacted in the fate of Jesus. For Cox the category of the kingdom is actualized when and as secularization and politicization of this world take place in man's responsible activity. The dynamic of the future which makes itself felt in action in the present comes not from a future reality but from the reality of the open-endedness of the present.

Pannenberg's emphasis on a future reality in contrast to Cox's open-ended present in no way diminishes the effectiveness of the future in transforming the present world structure. The future of the kingdom releases a dynamic upon the present which not only de-ultimatizes the institutions of the present but also, as importantly, de-ultimatizes the actions of man in the present. Pannenberg's emphasis realizes the perfection of that toward which man tends rather than a perfection inherent in the tendency.

Pannenberg insists that "it is part of the very *condition* of true humanity, in the present provisional state of reality, to understand that no form of human life is exclusively and ultimately the realization of humanity."[36] The kingdom for Pannenberg is still emphatically the kingdom of *God*, and the recognition of this by man is still the presupposition of his humanity. Man degrades himself when he falls victim to illusions about his power. The kingdom of God is not the present reality. It still remains to the Christian community in its preliminary function to be possessed by an inspiration—an inspiration realized, though imperfectly—which ever renews "our striving in devotion to history's destiny" in the future coming kingdom.

This concept of the kingdom of God constantly stands in judgment upon every aspect of the present at the same time that it moves the present toward its proper future. This judging function is precisely what is missing in Cox's pronouncements of secularization. And this lack makes it impossible for Cox to de-ultimatize his own thought. While Pannenberg can be thankful for some of the insights of Cox's secularity, he remains unimpressed by a relativistic approach that is unable to relativize its own formulations. It is only the future reality of the kingdom of God which can provide the judgment necessary to prevent present change from becoming absolute.

*Summary*

Once again we see Pannenberg's insistence upon a certain type of reality setting him apart from a prominent theological position. His emphasis upon a historical future reality in contrast to the power of the mere idea of the future for transforming or changing the present sets him apart from political theology. It does not mean, however, that Pannenberg is not appreciative of many emphases of political theology.

While Pannenberg agrees on theology's need for a cultural point of contact, he cannot accept Bloch's ontology of "not-yet-being" as normative for Christian understanding. Because God reveals *himself* through the historical process, Pannenberg as a theologian insists upon a reality that has a fixed point of reference. This point of reference is God himself in his future. Although historical reality is not yet what it will be, it is directed by the complete future of God and not strictly by man's hope.

Pannenberg differs from the theologies building upon Bloch's thought. He cannot accept Moltmann's affirmation that theology has to do with transforming reality. To make this the primary goal of theology is to accept the idea that the reality about which theology concerns itself is that tendency of the present to become the future. To Pannenberg the future as God's future becomes the present precisely because the future has a reality of its own; that is, the future is a reality that includes and continually revises the present.

Pannenberg's disagreement with Cox centers upon a lack of judgment upon man's efforts to change his world. Pannenberg agrees that man is responsible for this world, but without a basis of judgment man cannot but absolutize his responsibility to change the world. Pannenberg's concept of the reality of the future is able to supply a basis of judgment upon the present at the same time it supplies a dynamic for man's responsibility. In so doing Pannenberg avoids Cox's weakness.

Thus political theology, while certainly having more affinity with Pannenberg's thought than hermeneutical theology, is still inadequate. For Pannenberg any attempt at a theology which centers its primary interest in the polis violates its own proper subject matter—God himself.

## BIBLICAL LITERALISM

The theological position hesitantly entitled biblical literalism deserves some brief mention, particularly in light of the fact that it has at times given a semiendorsement to Pannenberg. A chief tenet of this particular theological position is that the whole Bible is revelation in such fashion that "divine revelation is given objectively in concepts and words." [37] Revelation has to do with the actuality of whatever historical events are reported by the words of the Bible. Thus the historicity of the resurrection as reported in the words of Scripture becomes a prime datum for apologetical and theological purposes.

Pannenberg has upon occasion received favorable mention from this position for his view of the historical nature of the resurrection. For example, Clark H. Pinnock writes: "In his attempt to ground the event in history, Pannenberg is being faithful to the intent of the New Testament itself." [38] In the same article, however, Pinnock expresses "pause" with regard to Pannenberg's belief that there are certain legendary elements contained in the resurrection narratives.

The fact of some difficulty in accepting Pannenberg's idea of the resurrection's historicity encourages a closer look at the supposed affinity between Pannenberg and biblical literalism. As Pannenberg says, "Ambiguities of language often indicate a problematic subject matter." [39] This is the case with the word *historicity*. For biblical literalism, historicity is seen as a function of the already assumed identity between revelation and the Bible. Since God speaks and presumably speaks the truth, the account of the resurrection is already taken to be true. Historicity is affirmed not from a historical perspective but from a revealed one. The need for an approach to the resurrection through the historical method is not for the purpose of ascertaining the actuality of a historical event but rather for the purpose of providing "sufficient" proof to "encourage any honest seeker to examine the New Testament data for himself." [40]

The traditional ugly ditch between fact and faith is only a pseudoditch for the believer, since already faith has assured the results of the historical question. For biblical literalism, faith has already given an affirmative answer to the question "Did it happen?" Any historical investigation is strictly for the purpose of removing obstacles for the unbeliever. It is never for the purpose of establishing faith—a faith already accomplished in the equation of revelation and the Bible.

In contrast, historicity for Pannenberg has a more serious and radical significance. He intends to ask the historical question of facticity, that is, to risk the fact of the resurrection upon historical verification—a possibility excluded a priori by biblical literalism. Since for Pannenberg the historicity of the resurrection forms the foundation for faith and serves as the key to reality, he is willing to risk faith itself on the historical question. This is a risk biblical literalism cannot and has not been willing to take.

Too facile an adoption, then, of Pannenberg's theological thought concerning the historicity of the resurrection suggests a failure to come to terms with the entirety of his understanding of the nature and purpose of historicity. On occasion biblical literalism has been guilty of this failure.

## PANNENBERG: THE THEOLOGIAN

The mark of the able theologian or philosopher is the ability to make and sustain distinctions in his subject matter—an ability that Pannenberg possesses in abundance. For this reason he is not to be easily characterized by any particular type of theology. He is not primarily interested in pushing ahead to think through or further develop this or that set of assumptions belonging to a particular branch of the theological scene. Pannenberg rather is interested in being the complete theologian—complete in the sense that he must critically develop his thought from his own assumptions. Pannenberg relies upon his predecessors and contemporaries; but he is not a systematizer, developer, or schoolman of another's thought. He rather directs his efforts toward searching out and developing his own theological assumptions.

Some of Pannenberg's theological formulations appear at first to place him in this or that school of theology, but upon closer examination of the assumptions lying behind these formulations, the apparent similarities melt away into the originality of Pannenberg's entire thought system. Some elements of his thought which seem simple—at least simple in the sense that one can outline the derivation of some particular element from the broader theological perspective— reveal a complexity upon further study that reminds the student of the dangers of hasty generalization. All this indicates, as we come to summarize and conclude Pannenberg's place in the theological spectrum, the difficulty in placing him at all. Better perhaps simply to remind ourselves that common elements often belie radical differences, and in many instances apparent differences can speak of commonly held assumptions.

Despite his acceptance of some of the central concerns of hermeneutical theology, we have seen how Pannenberg can be placed opposite the two main divisions of this theology. He does not follow the solutions offered by "word theology," but then neither can he be placed in the typical camp of hermeneutical theology which concerns itself with a special kind of salvational history. In fact Pannenberg poses a third alternative to word and history—an alternative which comes through but yet breaks the usual bounds of hermeneutical theology.

Neither does political theology fare any better as a home for Pannenberg's thought. The primacy of the future, the God of hope, and the contingency of reality—all these categories point to a position apparently in basic agreement with

Ernst Bloch's ontology of "not-yet-being" and those theologians who use Bloch as the cultural point of contact. But again, apparent agreement dissolves, as closer analysis shows that what Pannenberg means by the future, hope, and contingency derives more basically from his own assumptions than from Bloch's. Upon occasion Pannenberg's concepts actually stand in opposition to similar concepts in political theology. Thus the attempt to identify Pannenberg with another focus of theological thought fails.

How then does the thought of Pannenberg engage present theology? As has been indicated, certainly not by locating him within any one theological position. Pannenberg's relationship to present theology is more nearly that of offering an alternative to the current theological modes. This alternative will no doubt incorporate many of the strengths of the other positions, while at the same time imparting to theological activity a direction which is answerable to the demands of theology's subject matter and task. I offer this merely as a general and hesitant suggestion. It must remain such until Pannenberg, his disciples, and his critics more fully develop the somewhat different assumptions inherent in his thought.

# IV. Pannenberg
# in Perspective

It is not surprising that a theologian as innovative as Pannenberg comes in for a considerable amount of criticism. Fitting no particular school of thought, he receives a fair share of criticism from all. Since he advocates an older philosophical tradition, that of German idealism, he is sometimes dismissed out of hand. Often the critic is reluctant to come to grips with a renewed expression of this older tradition. Because of surface similarities with various thought patterns, old and new, Pannenberg sometimes receives criticisms that miss the point, precisely because his critics fail to realize that surface similarities are seldom accurate indicators of identity of thought. While some criticisms go directly to crucial issues, others rather foggily grope here and there, unable to decide just exactly what to object to.

It is decidedly not my purpose here to either answer or reinforce the various criticisms of Pannenberg's thought. Some criticisms have been well taken, to the extent that Pannenberg has clarified—if not modified—his thought in light of them. Others have centered upon such vital issues that the discussion continues up to the present with a resultant proliferation of highly technical theological give-and-take. Again it is not my purpose to present—much less resolve— all the intricacies of these theological disputations. Besides, Pannenberg is well able himself to give answer to his critics. My purpose is to seek to penetrate the inner dynamics of Pannenberg's thought with an eye to determining how and to what extent he is actually a "maker of the modern theological mind." To do so necessarily involves some contact with the technical disputes between theologian and theologian. These will be discussed as necessary. Of more importance for this evaluation of Pannenberg's thought is the engagement of his thought with a more general understanding of the Christian faith. A theologian must not think and formulate primarily for other theologians. He always has a constituency, the Christian community, to which his thought must answer and relate. How well and to what extent Pannenberg accomplishes this is our concern.

## FAITH AND REASON

Problems which continue to exercise theology from generation to generation are likely to be markers of key issues for the Christian community's self-understanding. One of these problems is that of determining what relationship exists between faith and reason. Traditionally both have been affirmed as means of entrance into real knowledge. This raises the question then as to priority and credentials. Is one prior to and superior to the other? Theologians have given differing answers.

One approach taken to this problem is that of Augustine and Anselm, two outstanding Christian thinkers. Perhaps Anselm gives the best statement of this approach.

I do not attempt, O Lord, to penetrate Thy profundity, for I deem my intellect in no way sufficient thereunto, but I desire to understand in some degree Thy truth, which my heart believes and loves. For I do not seek to understand, in order that I may believe; but I believe, that I may understand. For I believe this too, that unless I believed, I should not understand.[1]

Anselm's concept of the relation between faith and reason is often described as "faith seeking understanding."

Here it is evident that faith is given both priority and supremacy over reason with regard to matters of Christian understanding. Faith precedes all reflection and discussion. Unless one believes he cannot properly understand. Faith is to the Christian as perception is to everyday experience. The blind man can have no clear idea of light and lighted objects because he cannot perceive them. The deaf man can have no clear understanding of sound because he cannot hear. Likewise the one who does not believe does not perceive, and not to perceive is not to understand.

So, according to this approach, reason is subordinated to faith as a way of knowing. Reason may have its legitimate province in the natural sciences or as a handmaiden to faith, but for the Christian, reason operates within strictly defined areas. Reason's task is to develop and explore that which is already most assuredly known through faith. Anselm outlines the correct order. "As the right order requires us to believe the deep things of Christian faith before we undertake to discuss them by reason; so to my mind it appears a neglect if, after we are established in the faith, we do not seek to understand what we believe." [2]

The second approach to the relation between faith and reason is that demonstrated best by Thomas Aquinas. To a great extent Aquinas would agree with Anselm's emphasis upon the superiority of faith. Faith is still the best and only complete way into a salvational knowledge of God. Aquinas maintains, however, that it is theoretically possible for the activity of reason, unaided by faith, to come to some knowledge of God. But this knowledge is not a perception of the supernatural means supplied for man's salvation by God. It is incomplete and inadequate for salvation.

For Aquinas, incompleteness of knowledge should not be mistaken for falsity of knowledge. The human intellect in its present condition may be weak and deficient, but it is not wholly perverted. Reason has its place in discovering the knowledge of God. Revelation, however, is still necessary, for as Aquinas says, "The truth about God, such as reason can know it, would only be known by a few, and that after a long time, and with the admixture of many errors; whereas man's whole salvation, which is in God, depends upon the knowledge of this truth." [3]

For Aquinas, reason has its own autonomous sphere and activity. It does stand in need of supplementation by faith for salvation, yet it nevertheless is no longer strictly a handmaiden to faith. Reason can function independently of faith and can apprehend some knowledge of God.

In one fashion or another nearly all theologians have made use of these two approaches to the relation between faith and reason. Some have not been as perceptive as Anselm in insisting upon the need for the exercise of reason in exploring what is believed. Often this defect has resulted in a theological hodgepodge which substitutes heat for theological acumen and accuracy. On the other hand, some who have followed Aquinas' approach have lacked his insight into the necessity of revelation for salvation. For these, too often, the autonomy of reason is applauded as the way to God. Reason itself becomes a savior. But these are perversions that need not overly excite us. The better expressions have continued to follow the more balanced approaches of Anselm and Aquinas.

In as much as theology has generally followed these patterns in coming to grips with this central problem, it is certainly legitimate to ask of Pannenberg how his particular
approach fits with these traditional understandings. It is precisely in his approach to this problem, moreover, that Pannenberg opens a new front, marking him as something of an
innovator.

In Pannenberg's discussion of the relation of reason to
faith, he insists upon a type of dialectical or complementary
relationship between the two. Faith is not a means to knowledge, revealed or otherwise, but rather a disposition toward
God based upon the probability of certain historical events
known by reason. This probability is established by a historical method which is open to the rationality of all men.
Faith is not some religious way of knowing but is rather a
risk and trust of life upon the future which has been revealed in the events of Jesus' destiny—events which as a part
of universal history are open to examination by the human
intellect.

Reason on the other hand is not considered infallible and
completely autonomous. Reason may err in drawing out implications from past events. But such errors are the result of
not allowing reason to be properly informed by the events
which it examines. These events themselves have the power
of transforming reason in such fashion that it can correctly draw conclusions from them. Reason must always be
subject to its subject matter; that is, it is affected by the
events which it examines.

Pannenberg's understanding serves the Christian community in providing an alternative to the more traditional approaches. The use which the church makes of this alternative,
for good or bad, will be based upon the sensed needs of the

church. But we are justified here in raising the question as to just how Pannenberg's approach will affect the Christian community if used. Or perhaps more to the point, we should ask what potential gains and losses will accrue to the church upon the basis of Pannenberg's approach.

To the extent that the church is satisfied with a type of supernaturalism wherein orthodoxy is preserved by isolation and faith is severed from man's world, Pannenberg's approach will be viewed as unsatisfactory, if not a direct threat. This is not to say that supernaturalism is in error or is valueless. It is in fact the attitude endemic to the traditional solutions of the problem of the relation of faith and reason. As long as reason is subordinated to faith or operates within an autonomous but secondary area of life, the sphere of faith is necessarily seen as more important, secure, and proper for Christianity. An emphasis upon reason is seen as the abandonment of faith's sure knowledge. Faith becomes subject to the vicissitudes of reason's discoveries.

In light of the more traditional approaches, the Christian community may well choose to reject Pannenberg's approach to the problem. But such a rejection will involve at least two losses. First, the Christian community will thereby lose a possible revitalization of the mission of the church. Because of a self-imposed exile in a fortress of faith, the church has had few grounds upon which to approach modern man—no grounds in fact, except a demand for the unconditional surrender of rational activity, a demand which to modern man seems the more ludicrous in light of the advances made by scientific reason. Scientific reason has been able to offer the possibility of the majority of the former benefits of faith without recourse to the abject surrender of the intellect. Modern man is too convinced of this condition to agree to accept faith's demands for absolute priority. Thus a strength of

Pannenberg's approach lies in the fact that he restores reason to a determinative place within the Christian faith and thereby opens an avenue of approach to modern man, an avenue that often has been summarily shut.

The second loss is that occasioned by the truancy of the Christian faith from the arena of positive human concerns. For better or for worse the concerns of modern man for his world have become the silent partner of theology today. However the church chooses to relate to modern man, relate it must, or surrender the meaning of its foundation in the incarnation of God in Jesus of Nazareth. If it does surrender this meaning, it surrenders its God-given responsibility to enter into and inform every aspect of human life. It misses its reason for being by denying the public dimension of the good news.

The discussion of these two losses, however, is not to say that all the gains are upon the side of the acceptance of Pannenberg's approach. When Pannenberg makes faith to be entirely a trust based upon the historical evidence provided by historical reason, he grounds faith in evidence which can never be more than historically probable. Since the revelatory meaning of historical events is in their actual occurrence, faith which is only trust is subject to the results of historical investigation.

Although to make faith a means of knowing suffers from its removal from the world arena, this understanding does have the power and attraction of certainty. Faith believes, regardless of what facts may be adduced in the historical investigation of the normative events of the Christian faith. Historical evidence as the ground for faith renders faith subject to the relative probability of the happening of certain reported events. If historical investigation indicates a probability that an event such as the resurrection did not occur, intellectual honesty would require a complete reorientation or renunciation of Christian faith.

Whether the church can or will adopt Pannenberg's approach with its resultant lack of certainty is not a question that can be answered quickly or easily. It is just possible that in this nonauthoritarian age the church will have to take some such exposed position in order to be relevant to its task and true to its nature. This is certainly Pannenberg's understanding. The final decision, however, is still before the church and as yet has not been forthcoming. Until the time that it is, any judgments as to gains or losses to the church will have to be withheld. It is enough to say that Pannenberg has confronted the church with a challenging alternative. This is his task as a theologian.

One additional question concerning Pannenberg's formulation of the relation between faith and reason deserves mention. It is certainly to the credit of Thomas Aquinas that in positing the autonomy of reason to discern some things of God he recognized that man is not all of one fabric with regard to ability, temperament, or environment. Because of lack of ability, desire, or leisure, the majority of men do not approach God through philosophical understanding. The majority achieve a knowledge of God through revelation which is known by faith, according to Aquinas.

The situation may be much the same today. Though some men may be historically inclined and rationally active, it is quite probable that a majority still for various reasons do not live in a rational, historical world. Upon what for them is faith grounded in Pannenberg's approach? Do they perceive God's historical revelation by means of accepting secondhand the results of the theologian's historical investigation? Or must they work out their salvation in some way foreign to their own natures?

## REVELATION, HISTORY, AND REALITY

Pannenberg's concept of reality is another aspect of his thought which needs to be brought into relation to the self-understanding of the Christian community.

As has been noted, Pannenberg expresses a deep appreciation for German idealist thought, particularly that of Hegel. Using Hegel's thought as a base—but most certainly going beyond its limitations—Pannenberg embarks upon the task of outlining what he calls an "eschatologically oriented ontology," that is, a view of reality that is based on a future-oriented history. Pannenberg insists that exegetical studies of Scripture indicate that God's revelation of himself is indirect. God reveals himself through universal history. Up to this point Pannenberg's understanding differs little from Hegel's total mediation of history.

To stop here, however, is inadequate to the demands of the Christian concept of the uniqueness and finality of Jesus Christ. For Hegel, Jesus could be only one other event in the whole fabric of history. Besides this, without a historical future the present inevitably took upon itself the aura of the high point and summation of God's revelation. For these reasons, Pannenberg goes beyond Hegel to an indirect revelation which de-ultimatizes every present, precisely because the full revelation of God which takes place only with the end of history judges every present moment.

Pannenberg also restores Jesus to a determinative place in revelation as history. He cannot be only one among other events, although he is fully among other events. Jesus' history is the key to the proper understanding of historical reality in which God reveals himself. His history is the anticipation of the future of God wherein God is fully revealed. These understandings put more critical weight upon Jesus than Hegel ever accomplished. But in order for Pannenberg to place this weight upon Jesus' history, he must first outline its connections with universal history.

The first way Pannenberg connects Jesus' history to the warp and woof of universal history is by virtue of Jesus' fulfillment of and identification with apocalyptic understanding. Jesus' history takes place within this certain type of historical understanding. For the apocalypticist, the kingdom of God can never be limited to any present moment. The kingdom continually breaks open every present to admit the coming future of that kingdom. The result is that no present can be absolutized, and the full revelation of God which is always future continually judges and revises the revelation in history which has taken place up to and including the present.

This is the context in which Jesus' history takes place and is the concept which governs its understanding. Jesus' history is to be understood from the apocalyptic viewpoint as that revelation as history which breaks open and revises even this apocalyptic understanding. And for this reason, his history is definitely of universal history, at the same time as it fulfills universal history.

Some of Pannenberg's critics have argued that Pannenberg is misreading the apocalyptic attitude toward history, that the apocalyptic attitude is one of negation and pessimism rather than affirmation.[4] But even if the critic's interpretation of apocalyptic is correct, the criticism misses the point of Pannenberg's construction. In order for the apocalyptic understanding to serve as the category by which Jesus' history is understood, all that is necessary is an understanding of history which recognizes present history as an incomplete self-revelation of God, and this precisely because he has a future history where he is fully revealed. All that apocalyptic must affirm is that no present event or sum of events is the

sufficient and complete self-revelation of God. In fact, a negative appraisal of the course and nature of history may be
just as conducive—if not more so—to this understanding as
is a positive one. The true genius of history as the indirect
revelation of God is the fact that the content of revelation is
continually revising itself.

The second way by which Pannenberg makes the history of
Jesus determinative for universal history is by the connection
of his resurrection with the general resurrection of the dead at
the end of time. Jesus' resurrection is an event which is "out-
of-place" as far as the present is concerned; and yet, it is
strictly a historical event. It is an event which intrudes into
the present from what can only be understood as the future
where universal history is consummated. This understanding
is made necessary by the biblical connection of the resurrection of Jesus with the general resurrection which is future.

Thus, because Jesus' resurrection is an anticipation of the
future, that is, it is a future event itself, it serves as the key
to understanding historical reality which can only be known
fully when complete. Since God is fully revealed by the complete historical reality, Jesus' resurrection in its connection
with the end of history can truly be said to be the unique event
of revelation. In this way Jesus' history fulfills and revises
the insights of apocalypticism. It affirms the essential futurity
of God's self-revelation, and it becomes the means by which
the future impresses itself on the present in judgment and
transformation. In short, it is the key to reality.

Again we ask the question of how these concepts relate to
the Christian community's self-understanding. Is Pannenberg
merely constructing a metaphysical theory which at best remains a take-it-or-leave-it option? If so, it is seriously doubtful that much has been accomplished, particularly in light of
considerable contemporary skepticism concerning the validity

of metaphysics. But Pannenberg does not intend these concepts to be just one view among several metaphysical possibilities. He is a theologian and sees here a revelation which
carries with it convincing force. This is a given view of reality
with definable advantages over other views and also over non-
metaphysical views. These are primarily advantages for the
Christian community as it occupies its proper role and task in
history.

The first and most immediately evident advantage arising
from this view of reality is the ability to speak to man who
is becoming—within large cultural contexts—more and more
infatuated with the preeminence of the future as the true
dynamic of life. Whether it be in terms of the kingdom of
God, the perfect Communist state, the New Frontier, the Great
Society, or some more utopian concept, men are taken with
the future and are seeking to persuade others as well.

Perhaps the current movement toward the future is a reaction—and even perhaps an overreaction—to a lengthy
domination of man's thought world by the past and the present. Man has been told in connection with some of the more
limited ideas of evolutionary development that he is a prod-
uct of an interminable past in which there lurk all sorts of
apparitions to which he pays homage by means of the failings
and evils of the present. Or he has been told that the detem-
poralized present is the most dominant of the possible tenses
of life and that man's actual salvation lies not in understanding his semiconscious past but rather in experiencing and
somehow working through the existentially felt *angst* of the
present—the experiences of forlornness, anguish, and de-
spair. In reaction, today's man is seeking to recover Kant's
third question: What may I hope? [5]

But if, as is more likely the case, the contemporary emphasis on the future is not merely a reaction to other domi-

nant emphases, the Christian community needs respectable
intellectual underpinnings for the adventure with the future.
Ernst Bloch admirably provides a secular rationale—at the
same time admitting his dependence upon biblical motifs and
ideas—for the involvement with the future understood as
"not-yet-being." Pannenberg hopes to perform much the same
function for the Christian community.

Pannenberg's eschatologically oriented ontology takes advantage of the current tendency to emphasize the future. He
does not, however, merely present his thought as a means of
capitalizing upon this tendency. For Pannenberg a future
which has ontological status is a biblical category which also
has excellent philosophical credentials. Pannenberg's "eschatologically oriented ontology" posits a dynamic biblical view
of reality wherein man is a creature who hopes, that is, a
creature who lives actively and purposefully in the present
because of the future that is before him. The existentialist
views man as always and ever the same, a creature living in
an "eternal now." In this view man's nature and every moment of his existence is always essentially the same. Man
relates to whatever makes demands upon him in a static moment of existential decision, a decision made in an inward or
vertical direction. In Pannenberg's thought, man is shaped by
his openness to the future of God as he relates on a horizontal,
forward-looking plane. Man is ever-changing, or at least
his present is changing as the power of the future presses in
upon him. This allows for more positive possibilities for man
in the present, as well as allowing for the full dynamic of
hope in man's life.

Another potential advantage for the Christian community
in Pannenberg's eschatologically oriented ontology is the affirmation of a nonrelative view of reality that does not ab-

solutize any of the categories of the present. As has been noted, the relativity of Ernst Bloch and political theology is not much to Pannenberg's liking. For Pannenberg there is a finality about Jesus' history which supplies a constant. Because his resurrection is linked with the general resurrection of the last days, it is a future reality which will not allow the Christian faith to be interpreted strictly within terms of change for or transformation of the present. Only for a nontheistic theology or a secular philosophy would this approach be a live option.

Furthermore, Pannenberg feels a need for a transcendent standard of judgment by which man's innate humanism and utopian tendencies may be judged. An ontology of the future is no philosophical cure-all. But it does provide a ground upon which to speak to and of a world bound up in its own concepts of the present. It does not say no to the present, rather it seeks the real ground by which a meaningful yes may be pronounced.

A theology of relativity faces the danger of being swamped by the crassness of a future which can only be labeled "made in the present." Even hope degenerates into vested interests when it is projected from the narrow insights of the present. In other words, hope cannot live on its own interest. It cannot live without a reality that is hoped for, a reality that stands in judgment of hope itself. Hope is rescued only when it hopes in a reality that transcends hope itself.

Pannenberg serves the Christian community by providing this cogent philosophical background. He enables it to be true to its place in universal history. And he enables it to maintain the integrity of the central categories of a biblically oriented theology without surrendering its responsibility for modernity. Against the claim that the thoroughly modern

Christian must surrender—or at least must fully revamp—
most biblical categories, Pannenberg affirms that it is actually
in terms of these categories that life is truly understood.

The recovery of these categories is certainly an important
contribution to the Christian community, if that community
wants to continue in the conviction that the biblical texts are
important and normative. The history of the confrontation
with a normative text saturated with categories uncomfort-
able to post-Enlightenment man has been extremely spotty.
Something as unmodern and as oriental as apocalypticism
and eschatology has presented the church with a rather tick-
lish quandary. The idea of the future has ranged from pure
otherworldliness in Luther, to studied dismissal and neglect
in the nineteenth century, to embarrassed rediscovery following Albert Schweitzer, to transmutation into existential
meaning in the present. All in all it has been as much of a
problem as the New Testament idea that Christianity is open,
universal, and available. The later New Testament writers
opposed the first-century tendencies to make Christianity a
secret enlightenment for the few. Modern theology has not
always been as outspoken.

Perhaps it is too much to say that Pannenberg's efforts at
seriously reaffirming these and other biblical categories is
his chief contribution to the Christian community. It is, nevertheless, an important contribution at a time when the church
is struggling to remain true to its normative texts and at
the same time minister to modern man.

## A LAST WORD

In some ways one tends to be oversatisfied with Pannenberg's
theology. Theology of a rational bent has a way of being too
complete, of having anticipated too many questions, and of

having articulated too many answers. William Hamilton has criticized Pannenberg for a lack of mystery, surprise, and anguish—elements which Hamilton feels to be inherent in the theological enterprise.[6] Although it is well understood that a criticism of passionlessness is probably in correspondence to the critic's degree of disagreement with the thought criticized, Hamilton's point is well taken. There is in Pannenberg's theology an intrinsic rationality which leaves little room for mystery. This is not to excuse the considerable amount of obscurity which has disguised itself as theology in the name of mystery. Rather it is to say that there yet remains a considerable amount of the unexplained and the unexplainable which Pannenberg takes little note and has little room for in his work.

Gabriel Marcel, a French philosopher-playwright, has said that "what is peculiar to a philosophical investigation is that the man who undertakes it cannot possess anything equivalent to that notion given in advance of what he is looking for." [7] More often than not Pannenberg knows what he is looking for. But then Pannenberg is a theologian-philosopher, and perhaps Marcel's comment does not apply. What can be said of Pannenberg is that he is a theologian who adequately fulfills his responsibility to his constituency. The constituency will do well to listen.

# Notes

## Chapter I

1. For Pannenberg the proper concept of Christian theology is that of a universal science. If theology is less than this, it cannot be what its concept of God demands of it. In "The Crisis of the Scripture-Principle in Protestant Theology," *Dialog* 2 (Autumn 1963):308, Pannenberg writes: "A conception of reality in relation to God, such that it cannot be understood at all without God, belongs to the task of theology. And that constitutes its universality."

2. Wolfhart Pannenberg, *Jesus—God and Man,* trans. Lewis L. Wilkins and Duane A. Priebe (Philadelphia: The Westminster Press, 1968), p. 12.

3. William Butler Yeats, "The Second Coming," in *Collected Poems,* definitive 2nd ed. (New York: The Macmillan Co., 1956), quoted by Nathan A. Scott, Jr., in *The Broken Center: Studies in the Theological Horizon of Modern Literature* (New Haven, N.J.: Yale University Press, 1966), p. xviii.

4. Richard John Neuhaus, "Wolfhart Pannenberg: Profile of a Theologian," in Wolfhart Pannenberg, *Theology and the Kingdom of God* (Philadelphia: The Westminster Press, 1969), p. 28. Neuhaus points out that Pannenberg particularly sympathized with the student protests in Bonn over the enactment of the "emergency laws."

5. James M. Robinson, "Revelation as Word and as History," in *Theology as History,* vol. 3, *New Frontiers of Theology,* ed. James M. Robinson and John B. Cobb, Jr. (New York: Harper & Row, Publishers, 1967), note 31, p. 11.

6. Wolfhart Pannenberg, *Die Prädestinationslehre des Duns Skotus (Forschungen zur Kirchen- und Dogmengeschichte.* Vol. 4. Göttingen: Vandenhoeck und Ruprecht, 1954).

7. Neuhaus, "Wolfhart Pannenberg," p. 11.

8. These three men are so designated by Pannenberg in private correspondence dated 7 July 1969.

9. Gerhard von Rad, *Old Testament Theology*, trans. D. M. G. Stalker (New York: Harper & Row, Publishers, 1962), 1:105.

10. Ibid., p. 117.

11. Ibid., p. 111.

12. Hans von Campenhausen, "Augustin und der Fall von Rom," in *Tradition und Leben: Kräfte der Kirchengeschichte: Aufsätze und Vorträge* (Tübingen: J. C. C. Mohr [Paul Siebeck], 1960), pp. 253–71.

13. Ibid., p. 263. Quoted by Robinson, "Revelation as Word," p. 8.

14. See Karl Löwith, *Meaning in History* (Chicago: The University of Chicago Press, Phoenix Books, 1957).

15. Ibid., pp. 184–85.

16. Ibid., p. 197.

17. It is interesting to note that while Löwith follows the exegesis of Oscar Cullman's *Christ and Time*, trans. Floyd V. Filson (rev. ed.; Philadelphia: The Westminster Press, 1964), he comes to the negative conclusions regarding history most in keeping with Rudolf Bultmann in *The Presence of Eternity: History and Eschatology* (New York: Harper & Brothers, 1957).

18. Wolfhart Pannenberg, "Redemptive Event and History," trans. Shirley Guthrie, in *Essays on Old Testament Hermeneutics*, ed. Claus Westermann (Richmond, Va.: John Knox Press, 1963), p. 330.

19. For an indirect statement on the need for unity in the Christian faith see Wolfhart Pannenberg, *Theology and the Kingdom of God* (Philadelphia: The Westminster Press, 1969), pp. 72–101.

20. See ibid., pp. 93–99.

21. This is a term Pannenberg used to describe himself and his relationship to Barth in the private correspondence cited in note 8.

22. This influence is particularly to be noted in Pannenberg's *Jesus—God and Man*.

23. Wolfhart Pannenberg, ed., *Revelation as History*, trans. David Granskou (New York: The Macmillan Company, 1968), pp. 5–6.

24. Karl Barth, *Church Dogmatics*, ed. G. W. Bromiley and T. F. Torrance (Edinburgh: T. & T. Clark, 1936), I/1, p. 369.

25. Pannenberg, *Revelation as History*, note 14, p. 20. Cf. Barth, *Church Dogmatics*, II/1, pp. 73–74.

26. Pannenberg, *Revelation as History*, p. 5.

27. Ibid.

28. The *Habilitationsschriften* is a second dissertation required in German academic circles upon entrance into an academic career.

29. Pannenberg, "Redemptive Event and History," pp. 314–35.

30. Ibid., p. 314.

31. Robinson, "Revelation as Word," p. 13.

32. Robert Wilkin, "Who Is Wolfhart Pannenberg?" *Dialog 4,*

(Spring 1965) :140, states that the circle was originally composed of
Ulrich Wilkens, Dietrich Rossler, Klaus Koch, and Rolf Rendtorff.
Wilkens continues, p. 140, "They soon asked a young systematic theologian, Wolfhart Pannenberg, recently returned from studies with
Barth and Jaspers at Basel, to join them. Several years later a Church
historian, Martin Elze, and another systematic theologian, interested
primarily in social ethics, Trutz Rendtorff, became members." Against
this account Lothar Steiger in "Offenbarungsgeschichte und theo-
logische Vernunft: Zur Theologie W. Pannenbergs," *Zeitschrift für
Theologie und Kirche* 59, no. 1 (1962):89, comments: "The Old
Testament scholar Klaus Koch, and in the area of Church History,
Martin Elze, give less clear indication of belonging to this group."
Quoted by Robinson, "Revelation as Word," note 42, p. 13. It is
certain that by the time of the publication of *Offenbarung als Geschichte*, ed. Wolfhart Pannenberg (Göttingen: Vandenhoeck und
Ruprecht, 1961), the brother of Rolf Rendtorff, Trutz Rendtorff, had
identified himself with the group. Exact lines for the group, however,
cannot be distinguished, if they ever existed.

33. Ernst Bloch's primary work is *Das Prinzip Hoffnung* (2nd ed.;
Frankfurt: Suhrkamp Verlag, 1959).

34. Pannenberg's *Jesus—God and Man* goes back to his years in
Wuppertal where in the academic year 1959–60, he offered a lecture
on christology. Consequently, by 1963, when Pannenberg first read
Bloch, Pannenberg's christology was nearly complete. For the concept
of "anticipation" see especially Pannenberg, *Revelation as History*,
pp. 139–45.

## Chapter II

1. A blurb from the Westminster Press's prepublication folder on
Pannenberg's *Jesus—God and Man.*

2. Wolfhart Pannenberg, "The Question of God," trans. C. E.
Braaten, *Interpretation* 21 (July 1967):289–314. Pannenberg speaks
of the imminent possibility of speech concerning God becoming an
"empty word" even within the Christian world. Such a possibility has
arrived because of theology's retreat from its proper task, according
to Pannenberg.

3. Wolfhart Pannenberg, "Crisis of the Scripture-Principle," p.
307.

4. Ibid., p. 308.

5. Ibid. Pannenberg writes: "But if theology withdraws to a special
field, becoming a special science beside other special sciences, then the
universality which is connected with the idea of God is endangered."
This violates the intent of the first commandment.

6. Wolfhart Pannenberg, "The Revelation of God in Jesus of Nazareth," *Theology as History*, vol. 3, *New Frontiers in Theology*, ed. James M. Robinson and John B. Cobb, Jr. (New York: Harper & Row, Publishers, 1967), p. 131.

7. Pannenberg, *Revelation as History*, p. 135.

8. Ibid., p. 137.

9. Pannenberg, "Revelation of God," p. 131.

10. Pannenberg, *Revelation as History*, p. 136. The concept that the Holy Spirit does not serve as an a priori to faith has been that which has caused considerable criticism of Pannenberg. Most notable of this criticism is that of Paul Althaus in "Offenbarung als Geschichte und Glaube. Bemerkungen zu Wolfhart Pannenbergs Begriff der Offenbarung," *Theologische Literaturzeitung* 87 (1962), cols. 321–30. Pannenberg replied to this criticism in "Einsicht und Glaube: Antwort an Paul Althaus," *Theologische Literaturzeitung* 88 (February, 1963), cols. 81–92, in order to clarify his position. What Pannenberg is disallowing is not so much the work of the Holy Spirit in one's coming to faith but the attempt to justify one's faith upon the basis of a special illumination by the Holy Spirit. The Holy Spirit works to "enlighten" only in conjunction with the event of resurrection itself and not as some special "insight" available only to religious or Christian man.

11. Pannenberg, *Revelation as History*, p. 137.

12. Ibid.

13. Ibid., p. 138. There is no final separation of faith and knowledge, as Pannenberg makes clear in a comment in note 15, p. 157: "There is an existential movement in which both are bound to each other in a variety of ways. The knowledge on which faith is grounded is the present result of a process of knowing that is always open-ended."

14. Ibid., p. 138.

15. Ibid., p. 139.

16. For an excellent background study of the place of this concept in the current theological scene see Robinson's, "Revelation as Word and as History," pp. 1–100.

17. Wolfhart Pannenberg, "Hermeneutics and Universal History," trans. Paul J. Achtemeier, in *History and Hermeneutic*, vol. 4, *Journal for Theology and the Church*, ed. Robert W. Funk in association with Gerhard Ebeling (New York: Harper & Row, Publishers, 1967), pp. 122–52. See also Pannenberg's "Crisis of the Scripture-Principle," pp. 307–13.

18. Pannenberg, "Crisis of the Scripture-Principle," pp. 310–12.

19. Pannenberg, "Hermeneutics and Universal History," p. 130.

20. Pannenberg, "Crisis of the Scripture-Principle," p. 312.

21. Ibid.

22. H.-G. Gadamer, *Wahrheit und Methode* (Tübingen: J. C. B. Mohr, 1965).

23. Pannenberg, "Hermeneutics and Universal History," p. 137.

24. Pannenberg, "Crisis of the Scripture-Principle," p. 312.

25. Ibid.

26. G. W. F. Hegel, *Die Vernunft in der Geschichte*, p. 61. Cited by Walter Kaufmann, *Hegel: Reinterpretation, Texts, and Commentary* (Garden City, New York: Doubleday & Company, Inc., 1965), p. 254.

27. Pannenberg, "Hermeneutics and Universal History," p. 141.

28. Wolfhart Pannenberg, "Appearance as the Arrival of the Future," in *New Theology No. 5*, ed. Martin E. Marty and Dean G. Peerman (New York: The Macmillan Company, 1968), p. 128.

29. Martin Kähler, *The So-Called Historical Jesus and the Historic, Biblical Christ*, trans. and ed. Carl E. Braaten (Philadelphia: Fortress Press, 1964).

30. See Wolfhart Pannenberg, "Kerygma und Geschichte," *Studien zur Theologie der alttestamentlichen Überlieferungen*, ed. Rolf Rendtorff and Klaus Koch (Duisburg-Ruhrort: Joh. Brendow & Sohn, 1961), p. 129.

31. Pannenberg, "Redemptive Event and History," p. 333.

32. Ernst Troeltsch defined analogy as the "principle of similarity of all historical occurrence, which to be sure is not identity, but rather leaves all necessary room for differences, but for the rest presupposes in each case a kernel of common similarity, on the basis of which the differences are to be understood and tested." Cited by Robinson, "Revelation as Word," p. 31.

33. Pannenberg in his response to the discussion in *Theology as History*, vol. 3, *New Frontiers in Theology*, ed. James M. Robinson and John B. Cobb, Jr. (New York: Harper & Row, Publishers, 1967), note 75, p. 265, writes: "The instrument of analogy gains precision, if judgments about the historicity or nonhistoricity of events asserted in the tradition are based only on positive analogies between the tradition which is being studied and situations known elsewhere, but not on the lack of such analogies."

34. Robinson, "Revelation as Word," p. 32.

35. These theses are used as headings for the various sections of Pannenberg's presentation of the systematic conclusions drawn from exegetical studies of the Old and New Testaments by the members of the Pannenberg circle. See Pannenberg, *Revelation as History*, pp. 123–58.

36. See especially the sections by Rolf Rendtorff and Ulrich Wilkens in Pannenberg, *Revelation as History*, pp. 23–121.

37. Ibid., pp. 131–32.

38. Ibid., p. 134.

39. Ibid., p. 135.

40. Ibid., p. 149.

41. Ibid., p. 150.

42. Ibid., p. 151.

43. Ibid., p. 153.
44. Ibid., p. 155.
45. Pannenberg, *Jesus—God and Man*, p. 30. The other side of the christological task—the consideration of how the statements of primitive Christianity concerning Jesus came into being precisely the way they did in the process of the formation of the christological tradition—will not interest us here, not because this consideration is unimportant but because Pannenberg's own reconstruction at this point is dependent upon the more basic task of drawing out the significance of Jesus from his history. How Pannenberg accomplishes the first task of christology is determinative for the second. Thus our primary interest is in Pannenberg's approach to the history of Jesus.
46. Ibid., pp. 33–37.
47. See Barth, *Church Dogmatics*, IV/1, sect. 59.
48. Pannenberg, *Jesus—God and Man*, p. 33.
49. Ibid., p. 35.
50. Ibid., p. 98.
51. Ibid., p. 105.
52. Ibid., p. 90.
53. Ibid., p. 98.
54. Ibid.
55. Ibid.
56. Ibid., p. 105.
57. Wolfhart Pannenberg, "Did Jesus Really Rise from the Dead?" *Dialog* 4 (Spring, 1965) :135. This article is based upon the resurrection sections of Pannenberg's *Jesus—God and Man*.
58. Pannenberg, *Jesus—God and Man*, p. 130.
59. Ibid., p. 107.
60. See Pannenberg's *Was ist Der Mensch? Die Anthropologie der Gegenwart im Lichte der Theologie* (Göttingen: Vandenhoeck & Ruprecht, 1964). In this study Pannenberg elaborates upon the idea that the basic structure of human existence is openness to the world, *Weltoffenheit*. The religious interpretation of this *Weltoffenheit* signifies "openness beyond the given world," that is, openness to God. Thus this concept serves Pannenberg not only in defining man but also in formulating the doctrine of God. Originally, Pannenberg discovered the concept of *Weltoffenheit* in Arnold Gehlen's *Der Mensch*, published in 1940.
61. Pannenberg, "Did Jesus Really Rise?" p. 135.

## Chapter III

1. John B. Cobb, Jr., "A New Trio Arises in Europe," in *New Theology No. 2*, ed. Martin E. Marty and Dean G. Peerman (New

York: The Macmillan Company, 1965), pp. 257–63. Although Ebeling is more closely connected with the older traditions, Cobb still designates him and the other two as doing the pioneering work for future theology.

2. Rudolf Bultmann, *Theology of the New Testament,* trans. Kendrick Grobel (New York: Charles Scribner's Sons, 1955), 2:251.

3. Jürgen Moltmann, "Toward a Political Hermeneutics of the Gospel," in *New Theology No. 6,* ed. Martin E. Marty and Dean G. Peerman (New York: The Macmillan Company, 1969), pp. 66–90. Moltmann questions just this assumption, contending that only a "romantic organicism" makes possible the affirmative statement that the New Testament is normative for theological reflection. This affirmation lives off "the interest of the churchly tradition" (pp. 68–69).

4. Friedrich Schleiermacher, *On Religion: Speeches to Its Cultured Despisers,* trans. John Oman (New York: Harper & Row, Publishers, Harper Torchbook, 1958).

5. See, for example, K. Stendahl's program outlined in "Biblical Theology, Contemporary," in *The Interpreters Dictionary of the Bible,* ed. George A. Buttrick (New York: Abingdon Press, 1962), A–D, 418–32.

6. See Karl Barth's *The Epistle to the Romans,* trans. Edwyn C. Hoskyns from the 6th German ed. (London: Oxford University Press, 1933, 1968) and *Church Dogmatics,* especially I/1.

7. See various references in Barth's *Church Dogmatics* I/2, pp. 47–50; II/1, p. 265; III/1, pp. 59–60, for example.

8. It was this difference in outlook which was involved in the decision on Pannenberg's part to move from Basel to Heidelberg during his student years.

9. This subject matter is God as he has revealed himself through history. By so revealing himself God has laid himself open to human understanding.

10. Bultmann, *Theology of the New Testament,* 2:251.

11. Ibid.

12. See Oscar Cullman, *Christ and Time,* trans. Floyd V. Filson, rev. ed. (Philadelphia: The Westminster Press, 1964).

13. In supplying these basic principles of interpretation, Pannenberg follows H.-G. Gadamer's analysis of understanding involved in *Wahrheit und Methode.*

14. See H. Richard Niebuhr's posthumously published work, *The Responsible Self* (New York: Harper & Row, 1963), as an expression of much this same idea.

15. Paul Lehmann, *Ethics in a Christian Context* (New York: Harper & Row, 1963), p. 85. Cited in Harvey Cox, *The Secular City* (New York: The Macmillan Company, 1965), p. 255.

16. This statement is connected with an incident reported by Adolph

Lowe and described by Harvey Cox, "Ernst Bloch and 'The Pull of the Future,' " in *New Theology No. 5*, ed. Martin E. Marty and Dean G. Peerman (New York: The Macmillan Company, 1968), pp. 193–94.

17. Jürgen Moltmann, *Theology of Hope: On the Ground and Implications of a Christian Eschatology*, trans. James W. Leitch (New York: Harper & Row, Publishers, 1967).

18. See especially Moltmann's dialogue with Bloch in Moltmann's article, "Hope without Faith: An Eschatological Humanism without God," in *Is God Dead? Concilium*, vol. 16, ed. Johannes B. Metz (New York: Paulist Press, 1966), pp. 25–40.

19. Moltmann, *Theology of Hope*, p. 16.

20. Ibid., p. 18.

21. Ibid., p. 19.

22. Ibid., p. 21.

23. For an example of this tendency see Carl E. Braaten, "Toward a Theology of Hope," *Theology Today* 24 (July 1967), 208–26. Braaten does note the expressed differences and exceptions Moltmann takes to Pannenberg's thought. But these differences given by Moltmann obscure rather than clarify the very real underlying difference between the two men.

24. Wolfhart Pannenberg, "Der Gott der Hoffnung," *Ernst Bloch zu ehren* (Frankfort: Suhrkamp Verlag, 1965), pp. 209–25.

25. Moltmann, *Theology of Hope*, pp. 76–84.

26. Ibid., p. 84.

27. See Pannenberg, "Appearance as Arrival," pp. 122–28.

28. Ibid., p. 128.

29. Harvey Cox, *The Secular City: Secularization and Urbanization in Theological Perspective* (New York: The Macmillan Company, 1965).

30. Cox, *The Secular City*, p. 17. Cox credits this view to Friedrich Gogarten in *Verhängnis und Hoffnung der Neuezeit* (Stuttgart: Friedrich Vorwerk Verlag, 1953) and in *Der Mensch zwischen Gott und Welt* (Stuttgart: Friedrich Vorwerk Verlag, 1956).

31. Cox, *The Secular City*, pp. 21–37.

32. Ibid., p. 255.

33. Harvey Cox, *On Not Leaving It to the Snake* (New York: The Macmillan Company, 1967), p. 8.

34. Ibid., p. 12.

35. See Pannenberg's *Theology and the Kingdom of God.*

36. Ibid., p. 82.

37. Carl F. H. Henry, "Basic Issues in Modern Theology: Revelation as Truth," *Christianity Today* 9, no. 7 (1 January 1965):16. For a more detailed expression of this position see John H. Gerstner, "The Nature of Revelation," *Christian Faith and Modern Theology*, ed. Carl F. H. Henry (New York: Channel Press, 1964), pp. 95–109, and

Robert D. Preus, "The Nature of the Bible," *Christian Faith and Modern Theology*, ed. Carl F. H. Henry (New York: Channel Press, 1964), pp. 111–28.

38. Clark H. Pinnock, "The Tombstone That Trembled," *Christianity Today* 12, no. 14 (12 April 1968) :10. This article was written as an "editorial overcomment" to officially reflect the views of the editors of *Christianity Today* when presenting "A Dialogue on Christ's Resurrection," *Christianity Today* 12, no. 14 (12 April 1968):5–11, by Lawrence Burkholder, Harvey Cox, and Wolfhart Pannenberg.

39. Pannenberg, "Appearance as Arrival," p. 112.

40. Pinnock, "The Tombstone That Trembled," p. 6.

## Chapter IV

1. Anselm, *Proslogium*, quoted by Frederick Copleston, *A History of Philosophy*, II/1, 177.

2. Anselm, *Cur Deus Homo?* found in *St. Anselm: Basic Writing*, trans. S. N. Deane (LaSalle, Ill.: Open Court Publishing Company, 1966), p. 179.

3. Aquinas, *Summa Theologica*, Ques. I, Art. 1, found in *Introduction to St. Thomas Aquinas*, ed. Anton C. Pegis (New York: Random House, Inc., 1945), p. 4.

4. See for example Martin J. Buss, "The Meaning of History," *Theology as History*, vol. 3, *New Frontiers in Theology*, ed. James M. Robinson and John B. Cobb, Jr. (New York: Harper & Row, Publishers, 1967), pp. 135–54.

5. Immanuel Kant, *Critique of Pure Reason* (London: J. M. Dent & Sons, 1934), p. 457, cited by Carl E. Braaten, "Toward a Theology of Hope," in *New Theology No. 5*, ed. Martin E. Marty and Dean G. Peerman (New York: The Macmillan Company, 1968), p. 90.

6. William Hamilton, "The Character of Pannenberg's Theology," *Theology as History*, vol. 3, *New Frontiers in Theology*, ed. James M. Robinson and John B. Cobb, Jr. (New York: Harper & Row, Publishers, 1967), pp. 195–96.

7. Gabriel Marcel, *The Mystery of Being* (Chicago: Henry Regnery Company, 1960), 1:7.

# Selected Bibliography

## WORKS BY WOLFHART PANNENBERG

*Books*

*The Apostles' Creed: In the Light of Today's Questions.* Translated by M. Kohl. Philadelphia: The Westminster Press, 1972.

*Basic Questions in Theology: Collected Essays.* Translated by George H. Kehm. Vol. 1. Philadelphia: Fortress Press, 1970. Vol. 2. London: SCM Press, 1971.

*History and Hermeneutic* (with others). Edited by Robert W. Funk and Gerhard Ebeling. New York: Harper & Row, Harper Torchbooks, 1967. Sante Fe: William Gannon, 1970.

*The Idea of God in Human Freedom.* Philadelphia: The Westminster Press, 1973.

*Jesus—God and Man.* Translated by Lewis T. Wilkins and Duane A. Priebe. Philadelphia: The Westminster Press, 1968.

*Die Prädestinationslehre des Duns Skotus. Forschungen zur Kirchenund-Dogmengeschichte.* Vol. 4. Göttingen: Vandenhoeck und Ruprecht, 1954.

Editor. *Revelation as History.* Translated by David Granskou. New York: The Macmillan Company, 1968.

*Spirit, Faith, and Church* (with Avery Dulles, and Carl E. Braaten). Philadelphia: The Westminster Press, 1970.

*Theology and the Kingdom of God.* Philadelphia: The Westminster Press, 1969.

*What Is Man? Contemporary Anthropology in Theological Perspec-*

*tive.* Translated by Duane A. Priebe. Philadelphia: Fortress Press, 1970.

*Major Articles*

"Apostolizität und Katholizität der Kirche in der Perspektive der Eschatologie." *Theologische Literaturzeitung* 94 (February 1969): 97–111.

"Appearance as the Arrival of the Future." In *New Theology No 5,* edited by Martin E. Marty and Dean G. Peerman. New York: The Macmillan Company, 1968.

"The Appropriation of the Philosophical Concept of God as a Dogmatic Problem of Early Christian Theology." Translated by George H. Kehm. In *Basic Questions in Theology,* vol. 2. London: SCM Press, 1971.

"The Crisis of the Scripture-Principle in Protestant Theology." *Dialog* 2 (Autumn 1963): 307–13.

"Dialogue on Christ's Resurrection." [Reply to J. N. D. Anderson.] *Christianity Today* 12 (12 April 1968): 9–11.

"Did Jesus Really Rise from the Dead?" *Dialog* 4 (Spring 1965): 128–35.

"Doctrine of the Spirit and the Task of a Theology of Nature." *Theology* 75 (January 1972): 8–21.

"Dogmatische Erwägungen zur Auferstehung Jesu." *Kerygma und Dogma* 14, no. 2 (1968): 105–18.

"Facts of History and Christian Ethics." Translated by W. C. Linss. *Dialog* 8 (Autumn 1969): 287–96.

"The God of Hope." Translated by George H. Kehm. In *Basic Questions in Theology,* vol. 2. London: SCM Press, 1971.

"Hermeneutics and Universal History." Translated by Paul J. Achtemeier. In *History and Hermeneutic. Journal for Theology and the Church,* vol. 4, edited by Robert W. Funk and Gerhard Ebeling. New York: Harper & Row, Harper Torchbooks, 1967. Santa Fe: William Gannon, 1970.

"Insight and Faith." Translated by George H. Kehm. In *Basic Questions in Theology,* vol. 2. London: SCM Press, 1971.

"Ist Versöhnung unrealistisch? Stellungnahme zur Vertriebenen-Denkschrift der EKD." *Zeitschrift für evangelische Ethik* 10 (March 1966): 116–18.

"Kerygma and History." Translated by George H. Kehm. In *Basic Questions in Theology,* vol. 1. Philadelphia: Fortress Press, 1970.

"Die Krise des Ethischen und die Theologie." *Theologische Literaturzeitung* 87 (1962) : 7–16.

"Mythus und Wort: Theologische Uberlegungen zu Karl Jaspers Mythusbegriff." *Zeitschrift für Theologie und Kirche* 2 (1951): 167–85.

"Nachwort zur zweiten Auflage." In *Offenbarung als Geschichte.* [Postscript to the second edition in German.] Göttingen: Vandenhoeck & Ruprecht, 1963.

"The Question of God." Translated by C. E. Braaten. *Interpretation* 21 (July 1967): 289–314.

"Redemptive Event and History." Translated by Shirley Guthrie. In *Essays on Old Testament Hermeneutics,* edited by Claus Westermann. Richmond, Va.: John Knox Press, 1963.

"The Revelation of God in Jesus of Nazareth." In *Theology as History. New Frontiers in Theology,* vol. 3, edited by James M. Robinson and John B. Cobb, Jr. New York: Harper & Row, 1967.

"Theologische Motive im Denken Immanuel Kants." *Theologische Literaturzeitung* 89 (December 1964) : 897–906.

"What Is a Dogmatic Statement?" Translated by George H. Kehm. In *Basic Questions in Theology,* vol. 1. Philadelphia: Fortress Press, 1970.

"What Is Truth?" Translated by George H. Kehm. In *Basic Questions in Theology,* vol. 2. London: SCM Press, 1971.

"Zur Theologie des Rechts." *Zeitschrift für evangelische Ethik* 7 (January 1963):1–23.

## USEFUL ARTICLES ON PANNENBERG

Althaus, Paul. "Offenbarung als Geschichte und Glaube. Bemerkungen zu Wolfhart Pannenbergs Begriff der Offenbarung." *Theologische Literaturzeitung* 87 (1962) :cols. 321–30.

Betz, H. D. "Das Verständnis der Apokalyptik in der Theologie der Pannenberg-Gruppe." *Zeitschrift für Theologie und Kirche* 65, no. 3 (1968) :257–70.

Braaten, Carl E. "The Current Controversy on Revelation: Pannenberg and His Critics." *Journal of Religion* (July 1965), pp. 225–37.

———. "Toward a Theology of Hope." *Theology Today* 24 (July 1967) :208–26.

Buss, Martin J. "The Meaning of History." In *Theology as History. New Frontiers in Theology,* vol. 3, edited by James M. Robinson and John B. Cobb, Jr. New York: Harper & Row, 1967.

Fuller, Daniel P. "A New German Theological Movement." *Scottish Journal of Theology* 19, no. 2 (June 1966):160–75.

Grobel, Kendrick. "Revelation and Resurrection." In *Theology as History. New Frontiers in Theology*, vol. 3, edited by James M. Robinson and John B. Cobb, Jr. New York: Harper & Row, 1967.

Hamilton, William. "The Character of Pannenberg's Theology." In *Theology as History. New Frontiers in Theology*, vol. 3, edited by James M. Robinson and John B. Cobb, Jr. New York: Harper & Row, 1967.

Hefner, P. J. "Theological Reflections: Questions for Moltmann and Pannenberg." *Una Sancta* 25, no. 3 (1968):32–51.

Kehm, G. H. "Pannenberg's Theological Program." *Perspective* 9 (Fall 1968):245–66.

Neuhaus, Richard John. "Wolfhart Pannenberg: Profile of a Theologian." In introduction to *Theology and the Kingdom of God* by Wolfhart Pannenberg. Philadelphia: The Westminster Press, 1969.

Osborn, R. T. "Pannenberg's Programme." *Canadian Journal of Theology* 13 (April 1967):109–22.

Owen, J. M. "First Look at Pannenberg's Christology." *Reformed Theological Review* 25 (May-August 1966):52–64.

Robinson, James M. "Revelation as Word and as History." In *Theology as History. New Frontiers in Theology*, vol. 3, edited by James M. Robinson and John B. Cobb, Jr. New York: Harper & Row, 1967.

Steiger, L. "Revelation-History and Theological Reason: A Critique of the Theology of Wolfhart Pannenberg." Translated by J. C. Weber. *Journal for Theology and the Church* 4 (1967):82–106.

Wilken, R. L. "Who Is Wolfhart Pannenberg?" *Dialog* 4 (Spring 1965):140–42.

Olive, Don H.
Wolfhart Pannenberg

230.
044
092
OLI
C.2

| DATE | ISSUED TO |
|------|-----------|
|      |           |
|      |           |
|      |           |
|      |           |
|      |           |

Olive, Don H.
Wolfhart Pannenberg

230.
044
092
OLI
C.2